Table of C

WHAT TO EXPECT. WHEN YOUR CAT IS EXPECTING

An Easy Guide to Help You Get Through Your Cat's Delivery to Kitten Adoption

[Lauren Elaine]

Introduction

Is your cat expecting? Your cat would have been spayed in an ideal world before this occurred. Perhaps you delayed too long to spay your cat by mistake (life happens). Maybe you adopted a pregnant cat. In any event, she's now pregnant, and you want to provide her with the best possible care. Cat overpopulation is a serious issue. Please do not breed your cat on purpose unless you are a competent breeder with a purebred cat of exceptional quality and health. Because many disorders are handed down via heredity, your veterinarian should be engaged in determining if a cat is in great breeding health. If you're new to cat breeding, get the assistance of an experienced cat breeder to ensure you're doing everything right for the sake of your cat and her kittens.

If your cat is showing signs of pregnancy, the first step is to take her to the clinic. Sometimes it is still early enough to spay your cat. It is difficult to confirm a pregnancy in a cat until it is three to four weeks pregnant. However, if your cat appears unwell or exhibits unusual symptoms, you should still take her to the doctor for an examination and inform the physician that she may be pregnant.

Your veterinarian may be able to confirm pregnancy by gently palpating your cat's abdomen around three weeks into the pregnancy; however, this might be difficult if the cat is overweight or other signs, such as solid feces or a large bladder are present. If one is available, an ultrasound can be used to confirm pregnancy.

During the early to mid-pregnancy period, your veterinarian might discuss the possibility of spaying your cat and terminating the pregnancy with you. You may opt to do so for your cat's health or reduce cat overpopulation.

Your veterinarian may prescribe a radiograph (X-ray) 55 days into the pregnancy to determine the number of kittens expected. You'll be able to determine when your cat has finished giving birth or if she's in discomfort in between kitten births if you know how many fetuses she's carrying. Vaccinations are not suggested during pregnancy because they may harm the development of the kittens, while certain forms of rabies vaccination may be safe.

Your pregnant cat should be fed a high-quality, growth-oriented diet. Search for the AAFCO Nutritional Adequacy statement, which states that the food is complete and balanced for growth and reproduction. This is frequently some kind of kitten food. In general, wet food is healthier than dry food, although both are acceptable. It is always better to seek your veterinarian for their food recommendations.

Pregnant cats should not be overfed during the first several weeks of their pregnancy. Yes, she needs adequate nutrients for herself and her kittens. On the other hand, the kitten food includes the extra calories and nutrients she needs. She and the kittens may have issues if she grows overweight. After you have confirmed her pregnancy, gradually move to kitten food, but do not increase the amount she is fed unless she is underweight or seems hungry. Your veterinarian can help you monitor her bodily condition during her pregnancy. Feed her smaller and more frequent meals when she is six weeks pregnant. The kittens' strain on her stomach makes it difficult for her to consume much at once, yet she desperately needs the extra nourishment. Provide her with little meals four to six times each day.

Aside from modest vet care and dietary modifications, your pregnant cat should have no particular needs for most of her pregnancy. However, as she approaches queening (giving birth), she will search for a secure, peaceful area to begin nesting. Filling a cardboard box or laundry basket with blankets and hiding it away in a secure, quiet place in your house will help you prepare it. On the other hand, your cat may opt not to utilize it.

They'll do anything they want, as most cats do. Your cat may select the most inconvenient location to give birth. If you wish to keep some sections of the house off-limits for queening, make sure they remain closed throughout her last week of pregnancy. Also, make sure she has no access to the outdoors, as she may sneak away to nest somewhere you won't be able to locate her. As the birth date approaches, your cat may get restless and agitated. This is quite normal. Just try to make her comfortable and give her some room. Everything will be over shortly.

Once your cat has decided where she wants to give birth, you should leave her alone and observe from a safe distance. Fortunately, most cats require little to no human assistance when queening. However, if she is in distress, you may need to intervene. Note how long it takes between births, and make sure you know how many kittens to expect. Contact your veterinarian if your cat has visible contractions for more than 60 minutes without kitten delivery. Also, contact the veterinarian if more than two hours pass without the following kitten delivery. If a kitten lingers in the birth canal for more than a minute or two without being pushed out, immediately take your cat to the doctor. If anything else appears to be wrong, contact your veterinarian. Avoid separate mom and kittens for the first few days, and be sure you continue to feed the mommy cat, whose caloric demands will rise dramatically while breastfeeding and raising her offspring. Instead, take them all to the vet at about six weeks. If you do not breed purebred cats, see your veterinarian about getting your cat spayed as soon as possible. This is frequently done after the kittens have been weaned.

Chapter 1: Your Cat Is Pregnant, Now What?

For pregnant cats, further steps must be taken to ensure that she gets the attention she needs for conception and raising a litter of kittens. You may prepare your expectant cat for kittens by providing sufficient nourishment and safe habitat.

Caring For a Pregnant Cat

Confirm your cat's pregnancy. Pregnant cats must be confirmed before you may begin caring for them. Unlike humans, cats cannot do simple home urine or blood tests to determine whether or not they are pregnant. However, physical symptoms arise in the early stages of pregnancy that might alert you to your cat's possibility of carrying kittens. A cat's whole gestation period is only 60-70 days. Thus the process will be completed swiftly.

- The cat's nipples will get larger and pink by the third week. This is known as "pinking up."
- The cat will gain weight around the fourth week, revealing the pregnancy.
- Your veterinarian should be able to confirm pregnancy by the fourth week. A skilled vet can feel the kittens and the cat's tummy. An ultrasound might potentially be used to identify heartbeats.
- There will be significant behavioral changes, especially in the latter weeks. For example, they may look unsettled as their abdomen grows and meow for more attention or love.

In addition, they will eat more and sleep more than normal as their pregnancy progresses.

Pay strict attention to your diet. You must ensure that your cat receives sufficient nourishment for her health and the growing young inside her. You should be offering at least 25% extra food by the beginning of the sixth week. Also, a high protein and calcium diet is crucial for both the kittens' and the mother's ability to milk.

- Introduce a kitten-specific food to your pregnant cat. There is plenty of protein and calcium in these meal items, which the cat will need right now. You should continue to give them kitten food during their pregnancy and after birth.
- You won't need any extra vitamin or mineral supplements if you give them a portion of high-quality kitten food. Get a well-known and trustworthy brand to ensure that it meets the criteria.

- Make sure there is always fresh water accessible. This is as vital as any other food.

Maintain good health. Although a healthy cat is unlikely to experience pregnancy-related difficulties, it is critical to ensure that your cat is good enough to endure pregnancy and birth. Check your cat for parasites and make sure common immunizations are up to date. Other more serious issues to watch for are:

- ✓ If your pregnant cat loses interest in eating, be concerned. This might indicate a larger issue and a deprivation of essential nutrients. A cat may lose interest in eating immediately before giving birth in rare situations, although this should not last long.
- ✓ If your cat is being disturbed and licking her vulva region, there might be a problem. This might indicate that the cat is detecting discomfort or an issue. You should take the cat to the vet.

- ✓ An odd or unpleasant odor in your vaginal fluid should be investigated. This can occur during childbirth or throughout pregnancy and should be investigated by a veterinarian in all circumstances.
- ✓ If you detect blood in your cat's pee or if they squat with no urine coming out, this might indicate a uterine infection. If left untreated, this can be painful for your cat and impact the kittens.
- ✓ Ensure that your cat has a secure and pleasant area to relax. A secluded location is preferable, as long as she can quickly enter and exit the place.
- ✓ This private spot should be comfortably warm but not overly heated.

Recognize when the moment has come. If you've been following your cat's pregnancy since the beginning, you'll know when the due date is approaching. However, if you are unsure about the timetable, there are additional signs that labor is approaching. Among the warning indicators are:

- ✓ Your cat is actively hunting for quiet places to nest.
- ✓ Your cat is becoming less active and losing weight.
- ✓ A reduction in body temperature.
- ✓ Frequent licking of the abdomen and vaginal region.

Prepare for childbirth. It is critical that your cat feels protected and comfortable during birthing. This involves bringing them inside so they aren't exposed to the outdoors and making a secure and pleasant nesting space where they may give birth and milk their kittens.

Move your cat's current favorite bed or blankets to a calm and safe spot away from the hectic flow of the home. Make a nesting spot. This can simply be a huge cardboard box lined with her bed or linens. The mother will most likely start positioning herself in a nesting location a day or less before she is ready to give birth. If she picks a nesting location other than the one you selected for her, simply accommodate her choice by making it safe rather than attempting to transfer her.

Helping The Delivery

Observe and understand the delivery procedure. Giving birth to a cat is a completely natural procedure that she is designed to go through independently. As a result, you won't need to act personally unless there are indicators that the pregnancy is going wrong. Learn about the phases of birth so you may be better prepared to know what is natural. The first stage of labor lasts roughly 36 hours and is usually shorter if the cat has already given birth to kittens. Your cat will regularly return to her nesting area during this time, but she will also experience occasional contractions with strain symptoms. Further development of the nesting area, panting, and scratching is possible at this time.

Each kitten will spend between five and thirty minutes in the second stage. Stronger contractions will occur, and each kitten will be pushed out by vigorous straining of the mother, generally head first. For each kitten, the mother will break the sack and eat the cord herself, with no help from anyone. In the third and final stage, the mother will pass placental membranes and mass to each kitten.

The mother cat will consume the placentas to conceal that she gave birth. The complete procedure should take four to six hours. If it persists, you should seek the assistance of a veterinarian. Keep a look out for opportunities to assist. Although most deliveries go smoothly, you'll want to know what to look for and how to react in a disaster.

  ✓ If a kitten is only partially out and the mother appears tired and has given up pushing, you can gently assist the kitten in easing out, but you must be extremely kind.

- ✓ Alternatively, if the mother does not manage to bite through the cord, you can use a clean sewing thread to tie off the cable 3 cm from the kitten's body.
- ✓ Using a clean dish towel, you can clean a kitten if the mother cat refuses. Ensure that its mouth and nose are free of any liquids that might impede its ability to breathe properly.

Having a veterinarian on speed dial is a good idea, just in case. Problems may emerge, for example, during a woman's pregnancy. Only a veterinarian should be tasked with taking care of it. Contact a veterinarian immediately if you notice any of the following:

- ✓ Suppose the cat has been straining for more than 30 minutes and has not produced anything. A stumbling block might be impeding a normal delivery, placing the mother and kittens at risk.

- ✓ First and subsequent births can be separated by at least an hour.
- ✓ If the cat suddenly becomes frail and unable to continue working.
- ✓ The presence of profuse blood at delivery in the absence of a kitten. Greenish afterbirth is usual, but the absence of a kitten might indicate a problem.
- ✓ Keep an eye out for kittens that can't be moved with mild effort. A Caesarean Section may be required in some circumstances, and a veterinarian should be consulted.

Caring For a Cat After Birth

Continue to watch your nutrition. Your cat will now be responsible for her kittens. Nursing kittens will require your cat to have access to extra food, often up to twice the amount, and continue on a high protein/calcium diet. Continue to feed your kitten high protein kitten food and offer clean water.

Warm up the mother cat and kitten. To keep the kittens warm, the mother should use her body heat. However, you'll want to make sure her surroundings make this as simple as possible. Keep warm blankets around and the room temperature at a comfortable level. If the mother is not paying attention to the kittens, you can keep them warm with a heating pad set on low. Keep the kittens and mom in a safe location where she will not feel threatened. This might endanger the kittens and the mother.

Keep an eye out for post-birth problems. After the birthing process, your cat may still have issues. Consult your veterinarian if you detect vaginal bleeding or a prolapsed uterus (a uterus that has pushed out through the vagina). Look out for:

1) Always be alert for any unusual conduct, such as neglecting the kittens, and take action if necessary. For example, she may reject the

kittens, or if she feels threatened, she may murder the litter.

2) Look out for irritating mammary glands. Infected glands will swell, become hot to the touch, and even change color.

3) A shift in appetite should be noted. It's dangerous for your cat and her kittens if she isn't getting enough food. After not eating, take your cat to the vet after a long period.

Cat pregnancy is a huge event, and if you've made the big choice to allow your cat to produce kittens, you're in for a wild ride. A mother cat is typically more than capable of taking care of a birth on her alone, so leave her alone. There are, however, a few things you may do to make things simpler.

It is possible to tell if your cat is pregnant by looking at its behavior. Her heat cycle coming to an end might be the first clue. The swelling and deepening of the red hue of your cat's nuchal folds are further signs of being on the lookout for. Morning sickness may also set in for pregnant cats.' When your cat is five weeks pregnant, you may expect her stomach to start swelling and remain so until she gives birth. To sum it up, you could notice a dramatic adjustment in behavior. She can become too affectionate and eager to spend time with you suddenly. However, you may discover that your once friendly cat is now gloomy and withdrawn. Don't be alarmed; both of these actions are fairly common. Cats are known to give birth with ease. If you are concerned about your cat's health or want to confirm if she is pregnant, take her to the veterinarian. A physical checkup or an ultrasound will be used to determine your expectant mother's health and confirm the pregnancy.

Your pregnant mother doesn't need much help from you while she's in the last stages of her pregnancy, but it's important that she eats a healthy diet and drinks enough water. As soon as you know she's pregnant, move her to a premium kitten food like Hills Science Diet to give her and her offspring extra nutrition. Continue to feed her this food until the kittens are weaned. Don't be shocked if your mother cat doesn't appear to eat much at first. She has a belly full of kittens and would probably prefer to eat small amounts frequently throughout the day. As the due date approaches, your cat will most likely begin hunting for a quiet, comfy area to nest. Provide your cat with a towel-lined box and encourage her to use it. Don't be alarmed if she decides not to utilize it in the end. A creamy discharge from your cat's nipples indicates that she will give birth. A cat's body temperature usually drops to less than 38.9 degrees Celsius before giving birth if you monitor it. When labor begins, your cat may begin purring loudly, and you may notice contractions. Remember that a cat is perfectly competent in completing delivery independently in most situations.

The usual litter size is two to five kittens. A cat will usually wait anywhere from 10 minutes to an hour between kittens. You should take her to the doctor if you know she still has kittens inside her, and it properly took more than three hours to birth the last ones. When the kittens are born, they should be tearing out of the amniotic membrane or sac. If the mother does not assist them with this endeavor, you must carefully cut it open to release the kitten. A mother cat will lick her newborn kittens to encourage their respiration. It could be up to you if she's too tired or preoccupied with another delivery. Rub the kitten tenderly with a towel, just like a mother would. You should turn the kitten face down to assist drain fluid from its airway.

A placenta should appear after each kitten. If a placenta is retained, the mother may get infected. Count how many placentas you've observed for each kitten. Expect the mother to consume part or all of the placentas. This is very typical and secure. If the mother looks to have retained a placenta, get her to the vet as soon as possible.

The mother cat frequently chews off the umbilical cord. If she does not, you should assist her. Tie a length of strong thread around the cable about one inch away from the kittens' bodies. Make another thread loop about an inch up the cord, then cut between the two loops with a sharp pair of scissors. When the kittens are delivered and cleaned, they should immediately crawl to their mother's nipples and nurse. It's fine to give your cat and her babies some alone time at that moment. Congratulations on the arrival of your new cat litter.

Ways to Tell if Your Cat is Carrying a Pregnancy

Cats who haven't been spayed are more likely to give birth to kittens than those neutered.

1) **Physical changes:** A pregnant cat may have "morning sickness" and will normally eat more as the pregnancy continues. Furthermore, after around five weeks, your cat's tummy will be considerably larger, and

it will continue to enlarge until she gives birth. Her nipples may also get swelled and have a deeper, red hue.

2) **Behavioral changes:** Your formerly loving, the welcoming cat may go into hiding. In contrast, an otherwise disinterested cat may suddenly become a cuddling bug — both of these behavioral changes are common for pregnant cats.

What To Feed Your Pregnant Cat

If you find indicators that your cat is pregnant and your veterinarian confirms it, you will need to discuss nutritional requirements for your pregnant cat. Your veterinarian may advise you to return your cat to kitten food, which will give her baby nutritional benefits. As your cat's pregnancy advances, you may want to increase the amount of food you provide her to meet her increased caloric needs for her growing litter. Nevertheless, as the kittens grow older, her stomach's capacity will decrease, so feed her more regularly but less each time.

If your cat has pre-existing health issues or a sensitive stomach, consult your veterinarian before modifying her diet and feeding pattern. However, avoid too boisterous behavior near the conclusion of your cat's pregnancy. You will need to assist her in remaining calm as her date approaches since anything too energetic may trigger her tension. Keep an eye on her appetite and comfort level during the pregnancy.

Ensure that this birthing box is spacious enough for your cat and her litter and tall enough to keep any curious kittens from escaping! Place the nest in a warm location and line it with soft blankets or towels (that you don't mind discarding). Find a familiar area for the box that is quiet and out of the way, and teach your cat where it is. Your veterinary staff will assist you in determining the ideal checkup plan for your pregnant cat. You'll also be able to plan for the big day together. You must understand what is "normal" for at-home birth, and you must be prepared to securely bring your cat to the office if necessary, during labor. It's also critical to have the name, address, and phone number of the nearest pet emergency clinic on hand in case of issues outside regular veterinarian office hours.

Because your cat is domesticated, she may not have all of the instincts of a "wild" cat; yet, most cats require no intervention throughout the birthing process. Your cat may seek seclusion on purpose when she goes into labor. Most cats prefer to be left alone, and they certainly do not like to be petted or touched when giving birth. It's important to give your pregnant cat as much solitude as possible while keeping an eye on the delivery process for any symptoms of problems or suffering. Don't be shocked if your cat chooses to give birth somewhere other than the "nest" you've set up for mom and her kittens. If this happens, don't be scared to place the kittens in the box you prepared after they've been born. Picking up and handling newborn kittens is entirely OK; gently touching them will not trigger your cat to abandon or hurt her babies.

After your cat has given birth to her kittens, you should take both mom and her kittens to the veterinarian within 24-48 hours for a post-natal checkup. If your cat became pregnant by mistake, the post-natal visit is an excellent opportunity to consider getting your cat spayed to avoid any additional surprise litter.

Tips For a Healthy Cat Pregnancy

Extra protein and energy keep your pregnant cat robust. Standard adult formula cat food is fine for daily feeding, but it lacks the extra nutrients that mom requires. Giving your cat kitten formula provides additional benefits for her developing kittens. It will ensure that they receive high-quality milk, but it will also aid in their weaning process since they will mimic her and try some of the foods she consumes. Why not experiment with one of the following formulas?

Slowly transition your cat's food by gradually adding more and more kitten formula to her regular food over 7-12 days until the two foods are changed out. Taking your time will help your cat prevent stomach distress.

As your cat's pregnant hormones kick in, she'll likely become more affectionate and need cuddling. A pregnant cat needs a lot of love and devotion, and it's vital to remember that as her body changes, you'll have to be careful how you treat her. While it is safe to brush your pregnant cat, avoid touching her stomach. This is an extremely sensitive place, and any stroking there may cause her discomfort or harm to her unborn kittens. Avoid any noisy activities near the conclusion of your cat's pregnancy, and if possible, leave her alone. You must assist her in being as calm as possible at this time, and anything too lively may cause her to worry.

Before reproducing, your cat should have received all of her vaccines. Healthy moms pass on immunity to their kittens through their milk; therefore, it's important to keep her antibody levels high. Remember that if your cat is already pregnant and her shots are due, some vaccines cannot be given to her. Consult your veterinarian to determine whether immunizations are safe for both the mother and the kittens. Don't worry if your cat isn't immunized when she produces kittens. Everything should continue to go normally, but contact your veterinarian if you have any concerns.

Because worms can be transferred from mother to kitten, worming medication should be continued during her pregnancy. You should also continue to treat her fleas - just make sure that any medicine you use is suitable for her and her kittens. Oral illness can be identified by redness in or around the mouth, swollen gums, or foul breath. If your cat miscarries, she won't be distressed, and you won't know unless it's late in her pregnancy. If your cat miscarries later in pregnancy, take her to the doctor for a check-up to ensure she isn't infected.

While complications during labor are uncommon, a cesarean section may be necessary. This is true if the mom has had past pelvic trauma (such as a fracture) or if her breed is noted for having a particularly big head or body size, as is the case with Persians. If your cat is in labor but has been pushing for more than an hour without delivering kittens, she may require a Caesarean surgery. If this occurs, contact your veterinarian once away for assistance. Cats are far less prone than dogs to suffer calcium deficiency during or after pregnancy (eclampsia). To be cautious, keep a watch on your cat if she exhibits twitching, anxiousness, or agitation — these are all symptoms of eclampsia, which can lead to seizures if left untreated. Encourage your cat to stay indoors during the final two weeks of pregnancy to avoid having the kittens born outside. You may assist your cat in preparing for labor by constructing a 'nest' for her to use during and after delivery.

It is best to use a cardboard box packed with clean sheets, blankets, or towels. Make sure the box is large and tall enough for mom and her litter to fit comfortably in without any daring kittens escaping! Keep the nest in a warm, room-temperature location to keep her comfortable. Don't be startled if your pregnant cat decides to have her kittens somewhere other than the nest you've prepared for her. It is completely OK to handle the kittens once they have arrived; it will not cause your cat to abandon or hurt her offspring. Mum may pick up her kittens and return them to her nest once you've relocated them, but feel free to transfer them if you think they'd be more comfortable somewhere else.

The cat's fecundity has been recognized throughout its history with man; as a result, it has been revered by some and punished as wanton by others. When a female cat achieves sexual maturity and is allowed outside, an unneutered male cat is likely to discover her, and she will become pregnant before you know it!! In most cases, you won't even notice this until she gets fat and you're wondering what to do.

What Are the Basics of Cat Reproduction?

In most cases, the increase in the length of the day suggests better weather, and better weather means more food animals for the cat. In the northern hemisphere, cat pregnancies and newborns rise in March, April, and May and fall from October to January, but in the southern hemisphere, the opposite is true. Cats near the equator's reproductivity are unlikely to vary significantly over the year.

However, for female cats, this period of 'heat' or coming into the season, or oestrus, is divided into many brief intervals (each cycle is about 14 days long). For example, the cat will engage in "flirtatious" behavior like rolling around on the floor and making an up-and-down sound known as "calling." Owners who have never owned a female cat that hasn't been neutered may think their pet is suffering, but these actions are quite normal for a female cat trying to find a mate.

Male cats (also known as toms) that have not been castrated are continuously on the lookout for females (also known as queens) who may be susceptible to their charms! They will detect the female's scent, sound, and body language cues and realize what is going on considerably sooner than human owners. If the cats had access to each other, they would have married by the time we humans noticed. Even though a male in his area is more likely to win a fight with the female and have the opportunity to mate with her, the female may have other preferences. She will not accept any male advances till she is ready. She then adopts the lordosis position, in which she lifts her rump and rests her front end on the ground, waving her tail to one side. The guy takes her by the scruff (the loose skin at the back of her neck), and they momentarily mate.

In conclusion, the female cat almost appears to attack the male cat. Because of the barbs on the male's penis that face backward, we're not sure why, but the motion is likely to have a big influence. But, again, we don't know why.

Cats do not ovulate or release eggs into the fallopian tubes or uterine horns to fertilize like other animals during mating. So, to be fertilized, the egg must be released, and the stimulus is mating; in fact, numerous matings may be required to promote ovulation. A female may mate up to 20 times with a single male in four to six days. The cat can ovulate and pick the ideal male, one who is healthy and in his prime, thanks to this long period of receptivity.

For two days, eggs move via fallopian tubes and into the uterus, where they might be fertilized by many fathers, resulting in multiple fathers. Finally, the eggs are implanted in the uterus, and the resultant fetuses form two rows in the uterus's two horns. If no mating occurs, the eggs are not released, and the cycle begins again around two weeks later.

When a female cat becomes pregnant, her body alters gradually over the next 63 days as the fetuses grow. However, there is no apparent change in the first few weeks of pregnancy, and the first clue that owners may notice is a 'pinking' (becoming pinker in color) of the nipples, which also become more prominent. After that, she'll steadily gain weight, and as the due date nears, the milk glands will begin to fill.

The female's hormones also cause changes in her behavior, and she will begin to hunt for a decent nest spot to hide her offspring. Without the protection of a human family, the safety of her kittens is substantially less certain. You need a dry area and well disguised in the wild for the kittens' survival.

Even if her primary nest is endangered, the female may choose to build many nests to protect herself.

Owners may notice "nesting" activity in their homes (probably in the final two weeks of pregnancy). To raise her babies, the cat will look for a place that is quiet, safe, and, in general, dark. Owners can offer a cardboard box or bed with bedding if it becomes clear that this is the cat's favored place for giving birth to her kittens. The bed should be comfortable to snuggle on, but it should not be able to wrap the kittens in pockets or folds. Cats prefer to produce kittens in various locations, including cabinets, beneath beds, sheds, and even on their owners' beds.

What Happens During a Normal Cat Birth?

The female cat may get restless, purr, meow, or pant just before birth. Next, she will clean the area surrounding the birth route and teats. After the kittens are born, it is believed that the mom leaves a trail of saliva for them to follow to find a teat. Next, she will go through some phases of labor. It is well known that each kitten is born in an amniotic sac, which is suckered and nibbled upon by the mother. Next, she chews through the umbilical cord, consumes the kitten's placenta, and cleans and promotes her breathing with her rough tongue. Most cats (particularly non-pedigree cats) will give birth naturally and without the need for human assistance.

How Do I Care for Newborn Kittens?

By resting on her side and enveloping the kittens, the female encourages them to suck and keeps them warm. The kittens are led to her nipples by fragrance and warmth, where they obtain colostrum, the first type of milk produced and high in antibodies that help protect the kittens from illness in their early weeks of life.

While the kittens are sucking, the mother cat purrs - the kittens cannot hear when they are born, but they can follow vibrations to travel towards her. They have an inbuilt rooting or nuzzling behavior that allows them to locate the nipple, latch on, and encourage milk flow. They feed once the sucking reflex takes over. Kittens frequently return to the same nipple to feed, maybe to avoid fighting and to guarantee that milk is produced there since there is a need.

Kittens weigh around 100g at birth, but this doubles in a week and triples in three weeks. Cat milk is abundant in protein and fat, essential nutrients for this fast development. They first eat for several hours a day, pressing their mother's tummy with their paws to keep the milk flowing (the same behavior they may show on our laps or on a fluffy blanket). The kittens are completely reliant on their mother for eating, cleaning, feces, and warmth for two to three weeks. When they're four weeks old, they're using litter and emulating their mother's tray use; by six weeks, they're grooming themselves and building relationships. By four weeks, the mother begins weaning them off her milk and onto solid food, and in the wild, she teaches them about prey and hunting so that they may be self-sufficient as soon as possible.

So, if everything goes as planned, you won't have to do much for the first few weeks other than making sure the mother cat is properly fed and has the necessary facilities. This can be fed after the kittens are born and until they are weaned. When mother cats get unwell or cannot nurse their kittens for whatever reason, owners consider hand-rearing. If the kittens are little, this is a significant endeavor, and the decision must be carefully considered. Occasionally, kittens appear to be rejected, maybe because they are unwell or have a condition, and hand-rearing may prolong the misery. Thus it is not always suitable and requires time and experience to do it properly. Kittens are extremely vulnerable, and nurturing them may be tough, time-consuming, and unsuccessful.

How To Prepare for The Birth of Kittens

If you are one of the fortunate few who witnessed kittens' birth, you are in for a real treat. You can be there throughout the delivery and available for your kitten if any issues emerge as long as you're not too sick. The most significant element of this procedure is the preparation you perform ahead of time, starting towards the beginning of the pregnancy. Let's go through how to prepare for kitten delivery – make sure you have all you need at this joyful moment!

Food Changes

Like a pregnant person, a pregnant cat will benefit from a diet designed to keep her and her growing kittens healthy. Tracking her trimesters is one of the greatest methods to ensure she receives the proper meal at the right time. If possible, record the first time your cat becomes pregnant. You may feed your cat her typical nutrient-rich food throughout the first two trimesters. Then, you can alter her food to higher-calorie canned kitten food during the third trimester. This higher-calorie kitten chow will help her obtain adequate nutrients while her uterus is pushing up on her stomach, making less room for food without causing pain after eating. Continue to feed her kitten chow until she has completely weaned her babies. This helps ensure that she gets enough protein and calories during this physically demanding time of her life.

Emergency Equipment and Kitten Milk Replacer

It is good to see the vet throughout the pregnancy for a professional assessment (and congrats!). This can assist in ensuring that your cat is in good health and that you receive advice on what to do in the case of difficulty. Keep some dental floss available if the mother forgets to tie off a cord. Also, have some sterile scissors on hand if a similar situation arises. Although it is improbable, you can use a little quantity of iodine to disinfect the kitten's navel area if it becomes irritated or infected down the road. Finally, be prepared to hand feed the kittens if the new mother cannot nurse them. Obtain a colostrum-containing formulation.

Create A Safe Nesting Place

Your pregnant cat will be looking for a secure and quiet area to deliver her babies once she is near to giving birth. Create a specific nesting area to make it simpler for her. A basic high-sided cardboard box packed with soft towels, blankets, newspapers, etc. – essentially anything soft and pleasant that you don't mind being soiled – will be ideal for nursing. Just be sure that none of the goods you use has strong scents or perfumes. Kittens are born deaf and blind, and they recognize their mother exclusively via scent. Place her food and drink bowls immediately outside the nest and a litter box about two feet away. Make certain that the location you select is not a heavy traffic area. It should be hidden away somewhere secluded where dogs, other pets, and people visit only infrequently, if at all. Let it be if, despite your best efforts, your cat still delivers the kittens someplace else. She has instincts that she will follow regardless of your good intentions.

The arrival of kittens is cause for jubilation. You will be the proud guardians of a few new family members delivered safely and sound when properly prepared. When it comes to preparing for kitten birth, being sure to supply the queen with the necessary food at the right time, building a safe nesting area for her around delivery time, and having emergency precautions in place will all help guarantee a perfect delivery.

If you have a pregnant cat that appears to be ready to give birth to her kittens, you probably won't need to do anything other than encouraging her. You could even wake up one morning to find your cat has given birth during the night and is happily feeding her babies. However, although nature has a way of taking care of itself, you should be aware of potential issues when your cat is in labor and what you can do to assist.

Signs Of Impending Labor

Cat pregnancy lasts around 65 days, give or take five days. Take a look at your cat's indicators of pregnancy to see how far along she is.

- **Nesting:** Your cat will look for a peaceful and safe area to birth her kittens a day or two before labor. She may pick a location you provide for her or seek refuge at the back of a closet or under a bed.

- **Behavioral Changes:** Your cat may exhibit restless pacing, panting, excessive grooming (particularly her genitals), and excessive vocalization. She will also discontinue eating.

- **Physical Changes in Labor:** Your cat may vomit if her rectal temperature drops below 99 degrees Fahrenheit. The cat's nipples may grow, darken, or lighten in color in the days leading up to labor.

- **Active Labor Signs:** Contractions, uterine contractions that propel the kitten through the birth canal, may cause your cat to yowl in discomfort. A release of blood or other fluids is also possible.

Supplies For the Birthing

Your cat may choose to hide after giving birth. You may, however, make a birthing space out of a cardboard box or a laundry basket lined with towels or blankets. If the cat chooses this location, it will be simpler for you to see and attend to the birth.

- **Absorbent pads:** Line the delivery area with absorbent pads.

- **Towels:** To clean the area and encourage the kittens, you'll need clean towels or paper towels.

- **Nesting box:** Get a large nesting box for the brood if you've taken your pregnant cat to the vet and know how many kittens to expect. Although a cat can produce one to twelve kittens, the typical litter size is four. A 16-inch-by-24-inch box should be plenty for an 8-pound cat. The larger the cat, the larger the box required.

- **Heating pad:** Put a heating pad carefully in the bottom of the box and cover it with a blanket or several towels to keep the kittens warm. If the box lacks a cover, lay a clean towel over the top to keep the heat and drafts out.

- **Dental floss and clean scissors:** If the mother cat does not break the umbilical cord, it must be tied off with dental floss and severed with a pair of scissors.

- **Refuse bin:** After the delivery, you will have a lot of soiled towels, so have a washing basket, plastic bag, or additional box ready to dispose of them.

The Kitten Birthing Process

The cause of the birth process is unclear, although considerations include the uterus's size and weight, the fetus's size and weight, and the hormonal balances of the fetus and the queen. Rhythmical uterine contractions gradually intensify during the birth process to push the fetus out of the uterus and into the birth canal.

One kitten's birth might take anywhere from 5 to 32 minutes. By cleaning the kittens with her harsh tongue, the mother cat will encourage them to breathe. She will also break the umbilical cord by gnawing on it about an inch away from the kitten's body. She may also consume the placenta. The kittens will instinctively seek a latch on the nipple and nurse.

A rough, dry cloth can be used to clean a kitten's nose gently and mouth to help it breathe if the mother cat ignores the kitten while still in its pouch. If the mother cat has difficulties chewing off the umbilical cord, securely knot dental floss around it 1 inch from the kitten's body and cut it on the mother's side of the tie. If the placenta does not come out with each kitten, ensure that it does so within 24 hours after delivery. One placenta should be provided for each kitten. Counting the placentas is an excellent idea. If the placenta is still in the cat, you should consult a veterinarian. 30 to 60 minutes may elapse between deliveries, although longer durations are not unusual. Whether or not the delivery went well, the mother cat and kittens should be inspected by your veterinarian within 24 hours of birth.

It takes a queen around half a day to give birth to all of her kittens. The mother cat will relax between babies and should be allowed to breastfeed and clean the newly born kittens. If you've been keeping the kittens in another box, return them to the mother cat and assist them in finding a nipple. When she is not in labor, provide her food, kitten milk substitute, or plain, unflavored yogurt.

Problems During Labor

Fortunately, most queens can give birth to their offspring without the assistance of a person. However, certain difficulties are possible.

- **Extended contractions without birth:** Take your cat and any kittens to the clinic if you have more than 60 minutes of intense contractions with no improvement.

- **Retained placenta:** Even if the queen eats a placenta, count them all. Each placenta is equivalent to the number of kittens that were born.

- **Kitten lodged in the birth canal:** Breech deliveries are common and deemed normal, around 40%. However, contact your veterinarian if a kitten remains blocked in the birth canal for more than 10 minutes or if you detect green discharge without a kitten within 15 minutes.

- **Stillborn kittens:** It is fairly unusual for one or two kittens to be stillborn. Remove the dead kitten so that the mother can continue to give birth to the surviving kittens without interruption.

- **Postpartum hemorrhaging:** Although some bleeding is typical after giving birth, severe bleeding or hemorrhaging is a medical emergency that requires rapid veterinary intervention. If the mother cat is ignored, she may perish. Seek veterinarian help if the frequent bleeding lasts more than a week after birth or if it pauses for a day and then resumes.

All of the kittens in your litter should be cared for and fed by your queen once they are born. When your cat is nursing, her dietary needs will increase dramatically. Therefore, she must get lots of kitten formula. A high-quality kitten formula will meet your kitten's high-energy dietary needs. Something is wrong if your cat is not nursing or eating, appears in discomfort, or is sluggish. A bad stench and recurrent bleeding indicate an infection or a trapped kitten. If this happens to your cat, seek quick veterinarian attention.

So you've discovered that your cat is pregnant. This implies she will have kittens, and you'll need to be present for the delivery. Cats are excellent moms and are typically skilled (and, sadly, prolific) mothers. Feral cats worldwide give birth to kittens without human assistance and typically without incident. However, your cat is your duty, and she and the kittens' safety and well-being are dependent on you. So, a few weeks before the deadline, you must begin planning for the big event.

The most important thing to remember during most cat deliveries is to remain calm. Maintain your cool and avoid panicking. Your cat will sense your tension, and the last thing she wants during birth is more stress. The birth will be chaos. There will be some discharge, blood, and water bursting. The kittens will be born in a sac, giving them a rubbery appearance. That's very natural. To assist the kittens in breathing, the mother cat will tear the sacs with her teeth and lick them. Next, the mother cat will break the umbilical cord that joins the kitten to the placenta, and she will, indeed, devour the placenta and anything else that comes out.

While this article does not detail the delivery process, it is crucial to remember the above so that you are psychologically prepared for the sights and noises of birth. When you notice this, do not become alarmed. Do not yell, shout, or display displeasure to avoid stressing the cat. Stay cool and quiet, and be there to comfort her.

In a year, a cat can have how much litter?

As a responsible pet owner, you may either support her through the pregnancy, find excellent homes for the kittens, or spay her as soon as the kittens are weaned. You can take her to your veterinarian to visit your veterinarian and be spayed before the litter is born. Aborting a pregnancy may seem harsh, yet it can save lives because of the real problem of overpopulation and the fact that shelters kill hundreds of thousands of cats every year. There is no need to worry about your cat getting pregnant again until she is spayed. Due to the shorter gestation time in cats than in humans, they are susceptible to several pregnancies throughout the year. You may avoid unwanted pregnancy by neutering your cat early in her reproductive cycle.

Puberty

Like humans, the age at which a cat reaches puberty varies by genetics and environmental factors. This hormonal transition is comparable to human adolescence when your adorable little pet suddenly begins to display undesirable behavior. For example, depending on her breed, she may begin to howl or seek extra love from you while watching television between five and nine months.

Your newly crowned queen may damage your beloved furniture to claim her realm. So what triggers the metamorphosis of Dr. Jeckyll and Mrs. Hyde? First, of course, there are raging hormones.

Sexual Fertility

Like humans, the age at which a cat reaches puberty varies by genetics and environmental factors. This hormonal transition is comparable to human adolescence when your adorable little pet suddenly begins to display undesirable behavior. For example, depending on her breed, she may begin to howl or seek extra love from you while watching television between five and nine months.

Your newly crowned queen may damage your beloved furniture to claim her realm. So what triggers the metamorphosis of Dr. Jeckyll and Mrs. Hyde? First, of course, there are raging hormones.

Gestation Period

If your cat accidentally went outside during heat, there are a few possible pregnancy symptoms. The first indicator is darker and swollen nipples, which occur when your cat's body prepares to provide milk for its young. Her increased hunger and larger abdomen will be the second and most noticeable signs. As her pregnancy progresses, she may begin nesting by looking for a private location to create a comfortable birthing space. Look for her in laundry baskets and closet nooks. If you believe your cat is pregnant, make an appointment with your veterinarian for a short checkup and an x-ray or ultrasound. Some cats can have a pseudopregnancy, in which they exhibit all of the signs of pregnancy, including lactation, without really being pregnant.

Cat menopause is a myth, according to science. While a cat's fertility declines as she ages, reducing her chances of delivering many litters in a year, even elderly cats can give birth. In reality, animals generally have a life expectancy that does not exceed their reproductive years. On the other hand, pregnancy at a later age might offer health hazards to both the litter and the mother cat. Geriatric queens' litters and infants are often substantially smaller, and the stress of motherhood leads to a lower quality of life for senior cats.

When you consider how many kittens a healthy, mature cat may bear, the care of both mother and infant is intimidating to the average cat owner. This is usually reserved for tabloid headlines about cat collectors and backyard breeding ("kitten mills"). When irresponsible owners abandon unwanted cats in the street, these events frequently result in feral cat colonies. Don't add to the unwanted pet population by not neutering or spaying your cat before becoming a statistic.

Chapter 2: The Kittens Are Here, Now What?

You're undoubtedly looking forward to the day your cat gives birth to a litter of kittens. However, the enthusiasm may fade fast if you realize you're in charge of numerous delicate kittens and a new mother. As a beginner, start with baby care and learn how to care for them as they grow up.

Nurturing Newborn Kittens

Keep an eye out for complications during childbirth. During childbirth, keep an eye on the mother (queen) cat, but allow her some room. As a result, she won't require your support throughout labor or delivery. However, you'll need to keep a close check on things regarding medical matters. Here are a few things to keep an eye out for:

The kitten is still in the birth sac. The kittens normally emerge from their birth sacs, which the mother subsequently licks away. If she doesn't clean it up or rejects the kitten, you may need to massage off the sac with a soft cloth carefully. If in doubt, allow the mother some time to tend to the kitten first since she may reject the kitten. For more than 20 minutes, the mother had been pushing hard. This is a symptom that she is having trouble giving delivery. Check to see whether a kitten is halfway out. If this is the case, gently pull backward and downwards on the kitten using a soft, clean cloth. If the kitten does not come out readily, consult a veterinarian.

Similarly, if you see nothing, contact the veterinarian. After one hour, the kitten does not suckle. The majority of kittens suckle within an hour or two of birth. If this does not occur, gently position the kitten near the mother's teats to assist the cat in picking up the fragrance of milk. If the kitten is still not suckling after half an hour, gently open his lips and latch him onto a nipple to nurse. If the kitten does not eat after that, you may have to hand-raise it.

Make the mother cat feel at ease after giving birth. Because the mother cat will be the primary caregiver for the kittens for the first four weeks of their existence, make sure she gets all she requires. The mother will most likely select a nesting location where you can help her feel at ease. Place a box with clean, dry linen in the room and keep the temperature at the same as you would be comfortable wearing jeans and a T-shirt. You should also give the mother and kittens some alone time away from a constant stream of visitors, which might make her feel threatened. Room temperature is critical. Too hot, and the mother will grow upset; too cold, and the kittens will suffer from hypothermia. Newborn kittens cannot control their body temperatures and rely on their mothers to keep warm.

Provide nourishing food to the mother cat. After childbirth, the mother's food consumption will quadruple, providing lots of high-quality meals and supplementing her with vitamins and minerals. Kitten food is good since it contains more calories than an ordinary meal and has extra vitamins and minerals. Put food and water near her nesting spot so she doesn't have to leave her kittens. You should also place a litter box near the nest so she may relieve herself while being close to the babies. Kittens are born deaf and deafeningly deal. Their strongest sense is the scent, which they utilize to locate their mother's milk.

Prepare kitten food. While there are several methods for weaning a kitten (moving them from mother's milk to solid food), the simplest is to let the kittens follow their mother's lead. They usually start doing this at the age of four weeks. You may assist by leaving kitten food for the mother. The kittens may look simply interested at first, but as they expend more energy, they will begin to devour the food. It may be simpler for the kittens to begin eating soft food, such as canned kitten food. The mother will promote weaning by reducing nursing sessions. This will encourage the kitties to take solid meals.

Place a litter box outside. As they grow bigger, the kittens will begin to wander around, play, and eventually leave the nest. At this time, it's good to place a large, low-sided litter box outside. Show the kittens where it is to avoid further mishaps. It may be beneficial to have the mother defecate (or set some of her poop in the tray). This will alert the kittens that the tray is the designated toileting area. Clumping kitty litter should never be used. If the kitten examines the litter and consumes part of it, it may clump within the gut, resulting in an obstruction.

Keeping The Kittens Healthy and Social

Make a safe atmosphere. Remove dangers such as deep water bottles, strings, ribbons, or small toys to keep the kittens safe. This can prevent your cat from drowning or suffocating. You should also be cautious about where you keep hot liquids; if curious kittens knock them over and get scalded. Plates containing human food should also be taken from the kittens since they may consume food that causes stomach irritation. Supervise any other pets (particularly dogs) in the vicinity of the kittens and close up any areas where kittens may climb inside and become trapped. Also, use caution while entering a room with kittens. Kittens prefer to dart around unpredictably, making it simple to step on or fall over one.

Consider when to give the kittens away. Cats don't socialize as much until they are 12 weeks old, making it harder to acclimate to their new homes.

This interval helps the kittens bond with their mother and adjust to their new surroundings.

Check for fleas on the kittens and the mother. Examine their skin and fur for little black patches. Brush the fur and shake the brush over a white, moist paper towel. You may see red stains (from dried blood) and flea filth (flea droppings). If the kittens or mothers have fleas, consult your doctor for a flea remedy formulated specifically for kittens. Treat the mother, wait for the medicine to dry, and return her to the kittens. If your veterinarian discovers that the kittens have roundworms from their mother's milk, they may need to be treated with a liquid medicine (fenbendazole) administered by a syringe. This is suitable for kittens above the age of three weeks.

Inoculate the kittens. Consult your veterinarian to decide which immunizations your kittens require. Your veterinarian will advise you to vaccinate against feline distemper, to which your cat will be exposed. If your kittens are kept indoors, the vet may not recommend immunization against feline leukemia. This is because feline leukemia is spread through intimate contact with other cats. Even if the kitten will be an indoor cat, immunization is still recommended, and your veterinarian may advise you on which components are required and optional.

Make the kittens more social. Invite people over to hold and play with the kittens when they are three or four weeks old or are no longer continuously breastfeeding. This is a gradual introduction, so the kittens are not overwhelmed or scared (which could be traumatizing). Remember to expose your kittens to a range of people, noises, scents, and places before they reach the age of 12 weeks. Around this period, they find it more difficult to embrace new events and experiences. If you socialize kittens at a young age, they will be welcoming, confident, well-adjusted, and extroverted as they develop into adult cats.

Postnatal Care of Newborn Kittens

After a mother cat has given birth, postnatal care for her and her newborn kittens is critical, and observational skills are necessary during this sensitive period. Look for symptoms of health problems and kitten developmental milestones, including physical activity, in the first two weeks. Thoroughly inspecting for any irregular behaviors or physical looks will help you promptly identify difficulties, allowing you to seek veterinarian assistance.

If you haven't already, take the mother cat and kittens to your veterinarian for a checkup after one week. This is an excellent time if the mother cat hasn't been vaccinated. She may also receive roundworm medication to protect both herself and her babies.

New Kitten and Mother Cat Care

The kittens should be growing quickly, and if the mother experiences any postpartum issues, it will be around this time. Allow the mother cat to direct your attention. If she has been your pet for some time, she may look forward to your visits. A stray or foster cat might prefer that you stay away. The kittens will be OK as long as they are often feeding and appear to be prospering. Ensure the environment is warm enough because kittens can't regulate their body temperature until they're a few days old.

Ensure the box is large enough to accommodate the mother cat and her babies. Line it with clean clothes. As the kittens defecate, the towels will rapidly get filthy. The top towel should be removed first to show a clean layer. Keep the litter box, food, and water bowls of the mother cat nearby. Ensure she's eating high-quality canned kitten food fortified with

KMR (Kitten Milk Replacement). These specifically prepared diets provide the nutrition that a nursing, postpartum mother cat requires.

Kitten Developmental Milestones

Three days after birth, a kitten's eyes open, and the umbilical cord falls off. Their nerve systems are still developing, so you may observe them twitching while sleeping. This twitching is completely natural and signals that their nervous system and muscles develop. By two weeks, the kittens will crawl around and try to stand. During this stage, their teeth will begin to emerge. You may feel small tooth nubs if you put your finger in their mouth.

Using a warm, moist washcloth, you must perform this chore in her absence. The kittens should be wandering around and playing by three weeks. After that, you can start them on wet food and supplement them with KMR. They should still be breastfeeding aggressively. You can also get them used to using the litter box. Avoid clumping clay litter at this age. Any quality non-clay litter or the World's Best Cat Litter is ideal for young kittens.

Kittens are the most susceptible to intestinal parasites. Infectious disorders, including respiratory infections and congenital diseases, are common in young kittens. When a kitten fails to thrive, this is referred to as fading kitten syndrome. If you observe that one of the kittens is more sluggish and sleeps a lot more than its siblings, this might indicate the syndrome. A veterinarian who specializes in kitten care should see the kitten right away.

Postpartum Health Issues

Pregnancy, labor, and the postpartum period are all stressful times for a new mother's body. A new mother experiences a surge of hormones, milk production begins, and the recuperation process following childbirth is in full motion.

Unfortunately, your mother cat has a few serious problems to look out for.

Mastitis

When the mother cat's mammary glands become inflamed, it infects the milk ducts with mastitis bacteria. The teats swell and become hot, with visible "bruising," The mother cat may refuse to let the kittens nurse. Mastitis is considered a veterinary emergency. Antibiotics are frequently required to treat the illness in cats. Until the mother cat recovers, the kittens may need to be hand-fed.

Hypocalcemia

Although hypocalcemia, sometimes known as "milk fever," is uncommon in cats, it is a medical emergency. A calcium deficiency can cause this disorder during pregnancy and lactation. Seizures, staggering, muscular tremors, restlessness, and heavy panting are among the symptoms.

Uterine Metritis

Metritis is a serious uterine infection that is also a veterinary emergency. After giving birth to her kittens, the mother cat will normally have normal vaginal discharge. A foul-smelling discharge, on the other hand, is a red sign. Other symptoms include fatigue, fever, and a decrease in milk supply. The mother cat may need to be hospitalized and may require emergency spaying. As the mother cat heals, you will be responsible for feeding and caring for the kittens.

Has your cat just given birth to kittens? This is an exciting and hectic period in your home. While mom is busy caring for her baby, her body will undergo hormonal changes in preparation for her next heat cycle. Unfortunately, this is not the case. Most cats will have an estrus cycle around four weeks after weaning their kittens if it is still breeding season. So she might still be breastfeeding while also in heat. Estrus is defined as the phase of sexual receptivity and is associated with the generation of estradiol (a form of estrogen) by ovarian follicles. It is not to be mistaken with human female menstruation, and you will seldom, if ever, notice any indications of blood, but some mucus discharge may be visible.

As indicated in the term, induced ovulation, such as female cats do not ovulate without mating or any other external stimulation.

A cat's estrus cycle will finish if she does not mate at this time, and it will not begin again for two to three weeks. In her first postpartum estrus cycle, she's likely to become pregnant if she mates.

Eggs are viable (able to bear life) for about one day after fertilization, between 20 and 50 hours after mating. Fertilization occurs in the oviduct before the eggs go to the uterus, where they get embedded in the uterine lining. In the months leading up to ovulation, a female cat may breed with many males, resulting in a litter that contains offspring from various males. Two or more male cats may mate with an estrus-inducing female cat on the street, lasting up to 21 days.

Male and female kittens can attain sexual maturity between four and six months. Thus a cat could impregnate his mother. This is potentially hazardous for both mother cats and their kittens. Several recurrent pregnancies with brief intervals between births can harm a cat's health. In addition, carrying and nursing kittens deplete a cat's physical resources, leaving her hungry and tired.

Purebred cat breeders that practice responsible breeding do just that, limiting a female cat's number of litters and the time interval between them so that she has time to wean her kittens and regain her full health after each one of her litters.

The female cat will eventually be retired, at which point she will be spayed to prevent any additional pregnancies and allow her to enjoy her well-deserved senior years. If your cat has had kittens and is not a good breeding cat, she should be spayed once the kittens have been weaned. Meanwhile, restricting her access to intact male cats and the outdoors.

If your cat is not purebred, there is no reason to allow her to keep having kittens. Despite public awareness campaigns emphasizing the need for spaying and neutering, the United States struggles with a serious pet overpopulation problem. Most people choose to adopt kittens over adult cats because of the high demand for kittens. This leaves the adult cats homeless and at risk of euthanasia. The bigger the number of kittens accessible, the greater the chance of euthanasia for adult cats.

A female cat should be spayed after she has produced kittens and has weaned them. All kittens should be neutered or spayed by the age of four months. When kittens achieve sexual maturity, they can and will mate with their littermates. It's preferable if they're sterilized well ahead of time. Young cats being pregnant can be quite harmful.

Spaying or neutering your cats will make them happier and better companions in the long term.

Raising Newborn Kittens

Raising newborn kittens is difficult and time-consuming; it can also be profoundly gratifying and painful. To avoid the stress of dealing with the potential loss of your kittens, consider contacting trained professionals. If your hurting heart is willing to take up the task of stray newborns, go for it. Just make sure you have a place for them all.

Birth Mother or Surrogate?

If the kittens are strays but are being cared for by the mother cat, she will perform the task of raising them and, in most situations, will do a better job than people who try to step in and bottle-feed them. Bottle-feeding should only be a last option for kittens who cannot nurse. If the mom cat is peaceful enough to allow it, it is good to schedule a veterinarian visit to ensure everyone's health. Some stray cats are not used to being handled by humans, which may be especially traumatic for new moms. It is ideal for giving the mom cat enough room to feel comfortable while caring for her young kittens. Give the mother cat unlimited fresh water and food and a secure, quiet location where she may be alone with her babies. Ensure the kittens are all breastfeeding, gaining weight, and remaining warm. The rest is all up to her. If you come across newborn kittens without a mother or a mother who cannot feed them, you may need to step in and give the kittens their necessities to ensure their survival. At first, this demands round-the-clock care, exactly like bringing home a newborn infant.

First Trip to The Vet

Orphaned neonates should be examined by your veterinarian as soon as possible. Stray kittens can be infected with fleas and other parasites and may not have benefited from protective antibodies carried down through their mother's milk. Orphaned kittens may require some vaccines sooner than kittens who breastfeed until they are weaned naturally. In addition, any kitten exhibiting indications of illness or distress, such as low body temperature, watery eyes, runny nose, diarrhea, lethargy, or inability to feed, should be evaluated by a veterinarian right once.

Building A Nest

Building a nesting box for your kittens is next on your surrogate to-do list. You may use a large cat bed with bumper sides or a cardboard box coated with clean towels. Ensure your nest has tall enough sides to keep the young babies from falling out. This also helps the trash to stick together to produce heat. Because chilly kittens can quickly deteriorate in health, make sure the nest is in a warm area of your home. You may need to offer extra heat in the form of a heating pad set on low for the first several weeks. Wrap a thick towel over this pad and lay it at the bottom of the nest. Make sure the nursery also includes an unheated portion. If the kittens feel overheated, they will instinctively migrate to a cooler spot.

Feeding Newborn Kittens

Purchase kitten-specific formula, as well as kitten bottles and nipples. Feeding by weight should be done according to the guidelines on the kitten formula. Younger and smaller babies may require up to twelve feedings per day (every two hours), so set the alarm for night feedings and enlist the support of a family member. Bottle feedings can be done in a comfy chair with a warm towel draped over your lap. Place him on his stomach and expose the breast to urge him to suck. Feed each kitten until they have had enough and are no longer interested.

The newborns are ready to start eating soft food from a plate when they are three or four weeks old. Blend canned kitten food and formula until it reaches the consistency of a thick liquid in your blender. Prime each cat by smearing some mixtures on your fingertip and leading them to the dish. As the kittens become accustomed to their mush, gradually lower the quantity of formula in the combination until they are eating soft, canned food on their own. Your kittens may now drink water from a bowl as well. But don't be shocked if they play with the water before drinking it.

Your kittens will eventually progress to all solid diets, which may include a combination of canned and dry kitten food. Because their stomachs are tiny, feed them four or five little meals every day until they are eight weeks old.

Nurturing Newborn Kittens

The mother kitten undertakes various actions that guarantee her babies' health and foster bonding. These responsibilities depend on you as the boss. Mother cats bathe their babies' bottoms with their tongues to help them pee and evacuate their bowels. Holding each kitten (with a towel over your lap first) and gently massaging its hind end with a warm wet washcloth or the moistened cotton ball might stimulate the same elimination pattern. After each meal, you should be rewarded with pee and a bowel movement. Grooming and rubbing your newborn kittens simulate the bonding rituals that the mother cat normally engages in. To clean your kittens' bodies, use a soft baby brush, cloth, or soft bristles toothbrush to rub them down their backs and tummies. Soft-touch and massage assist kittens in adjusting to your presence and their new home.

Litterbox Training

Kittens are as fast to use the litterbox as ducks are to water. For training, use a low-sided box—the lid of a shoebox works nicely. For untrained newcomers, non-clumping pellet litter is best, as clumping litter causes gastric upset if they ingest it. When the kittens start eating independently, put them in the box 5-10 minutes later. Scratch the litter with your finger to demonstrate what it is. When they jump out, reintroduce them and then let them alone.

Taking care of a fresh new fur baby is both a delight and a huge responsibility, and it takes a specialized understanding of newborn kitten care. A kitten is considered a newborn from birth to four months, giving her enough time to be weaned from her mother and acquire a few basic skills, like eating and using a litter box. Whether you're the primary caregiver for newborn kittens or collaborate with a cat mom, prepare yourself with the tools to keep your new cuddle babies in top condition. Because newborn kittens are born blind (open their eyes between seven and fourteen days after birth), they must be kept secure and warm. If feasible, they will snuggle up with each other and their mother. Provide a comfortable bed made of layered materials, such as fleece blankets, and consider building a DIY cat bed to accommodate your cuddle pool of cats of all ages.

If the cat mother is not around to nurse, the infants must be bottle-fed with a specific formula. Best Friends warns against feeding a cat on her back because she might choke. Instead, turn her on her side (as she would when nursing her mother) or keep her upright. Give your small feline specially made kitten food once she has been fully weaned to help her grow strong bones, eyes, and muscles.

Litter box training is a crucial part of newborn kitten care. Cats aren't born knowing where to go to the toilet. Therefore it's up to you if mom cat isn't around to assist. Allow her to study the box to become acquainted with its location and function. You may need to stimulate cat mom's pee or a bowel movement in place of her. "A recommended strategy is to use a warm washcloth or cotton ball and gently clean the kitten's urogenital region until elimination happens," says Canada's Pet Information Centre. Repeat this every several hours until she learns the behavior on her own.

Brushing or combing her coat regularly eliminates superfluous hair (thus minimizing hairballs) and maintains it clean and shining, while nail cutting reduces the likelihood of a claw snag.

Experts urge that newborn kittens see a veterinarian as soon as possible, preferably within the first week or two of birth, so that the doctor may conduct a thorough wellness check. In addition, the Drake Center for Veterinary Care advises pet parents to keep a close eye on their kitten's food intake and record any "motor skills and coordination delays or problems, [or] lethargy, diarrhea, or vomiting."

However, a veterinarian may prescribe the treatment at an earlier age in some cases. Spaying a newborn kitten is not normally part of newborn kitten care. Still, if she's old enough, cat experts strongly advise spaying and neutering for your cat's health and to keep cat overpopulation under control.

Whether you plan to adopt or retain your kittens, you should socialize them as soon as possible. The Nest recommends touching your kittens one at a time once they've reached their first week of life and allowing the mom kitty to sniff you first if she's there. Baby kittens like nipping and pawing at their caretakers, but this activity can be dangerous as a cat grows. When a kitten is socialized, she feels more at ease and confident when interacting with people and other animals, preparing her to adjust to a new environment when she is adopted. Cats who don't like being touched will find it simpler to manage essentials such as toothbrushing, vet appointments, and meeting new people. A swarm of tiny newborn kittens is tough to imagine anything sweeter. These delicate yet lively tiny animals rely on you, their pet parent, for everything, and investing in a young cat's care and well-being will melt your heart.

Body Warmth

We must assist kittens under four weeks of age in maintaining body temperature since they cannot thermoregulate. This disk then supplies the required warmth for a further 8 hours. Each disk has instructions for how long to heat the Snuggle Safe disk based on the microwave's wattage. If you are unsure about the microwave's wattage, heat the disk for 5 minutes and verify the temperature with your fingertips. Before putting it in the cage or box, make sure it doesn't feel too hot. If no heating disk is available, lay a heating pad on the cage floor or under the crate, then place a gently folded towel or blanket between the kitten and the heating pad. Check the heat source regularly to ensure it is not overly hot or cold. Ensure that certain cage areas do not have a disk or a heating pad under them so that kittens may walk away from the heat source if it becomes too hot. Kittens enjoy having a comfortable nest in their cage or box, so wrap them in a soft fleece that they can burrow into and out of.

The importance of a heat source in orphaned kittens cannot be overstated. The queen would have given them a comfortable 100-103oF (38-39oC) atmosphere. Maintain a heat source for orphaned kittens until they are four to six weeks old. Although kittens over four weeks old may begin to shun the warmed bed, even older kittens may seek a warm location if the room is chilly. Consider suitably pairing new single kittens of the same age for this reason and socializing, so they may share body heat and be less likely to endure hypothermia.

A warm, non-drafty room is essential for creating a decent habitat for kittens. Provide a bed made from a mini-litterbox or food carton to keep kittens from sleeping in their litterboxes. A towel draped over the crate or front of the cage avoids drafts and keeps kittens under four weeks warm. Ideally, kitten chambers should be kept around 85oF or 29oC, although we understand that this isn't always possible. A six-week kitten simply needs a warm, comfortable place to sleep.

Kitten Feeding

Daily weight growth indicates that the diet provides the kittens' nutritional demands. Weigh kittens simultaneously every day to guarantee an appropriate weight increase and calculate how much they should consume with each meal. Kittens should acquire around 12 ounces (14 grams) per day or 4 ounces (113 grams) each week. Kittens are more used to taking milk from their mother's breasts when they are younger. Frequency is important for digestion since it helps the kitten's digestive system manage small amounts at once.

Cats that don't eat enough at one meal should either have more frequent feedings or be given another chance after everyone else has done eating. Kittens must be kept warm; if their body temperature is too low, they will not be able to digest correctly. 2 parts water to 1-part powdered KMR formula (NEVER give them cow's milk and continue to feed them the same formula.) Kittens should consume two tablespoons or 30 ccs of formula for 4 ounces of body weight every 24 hours. Kittens under the age of two weeks should be fed every two hours. Kittens from 2 to 4 weeks should feed every 3-4 hours. Do not disturb them to feed if they sleep for extended periods during the night. Feed weak kittens or those that aren't eating often enough. Individual differences in frequency and quantity may occur for each kitten.

Warm the bottle in hot water for a few minutes or in the microwave until it reaches the appropriate temperature. If you use the microwave, carefully mix the mixture before testing since hot spots may form during the healing process. Always feed a kitten in the appropriate position. While feeding, NEVER recline a kitten on its back. As a result, the kitten may aspirate, which means the formula is inhaled rather than swallowed by the cat. Reactive pneumonia can be dangerous if aspiration occurs.

They are most comfortable when placed in a nursing posture. A towel or cloth should be placed on the kitten's stomach so that the cat may intuitively knead on the material. Put the kitten in a towel and feed it if it's upset while breastfeeding. When bottle-feeding, gently open the kitten's mouth and insert the nipple using the tip of your finger. The kitten excitedly seeks out the nipple as it recognizes what is about to happen. You will notice a suction effect while the kitten is in suckle mode. Keep an eye out for the bottle's bubbles and the baby's ears moving while sucking. The kitten's sucking actions show that it is doing so efficiently.

Tighten the bottle slightly to prevent air from getting into its stomach while holding it at a 45-degree angle. Permit the kittens to suck whenever they like. You might attempt vigorously caressing the kitten's forehead and stroking its back in the mother's approach to get her to take the nipple or suckle. Using a toothbrush to stroke the kitten can replicate the sensation of the queen's tongue. If it still doesn't nurse from the bottle, a syringe feeds the kitten to ensure it gets enough nutrients. Prepare a strategy for who foster parents should call if a kitten requires syringe feeding.

When feeding numerous kittens, feeding each one multiple times during the session will make it simpler to have them all given the needed quantity. Feed the first kitten until it no longer nurses, then feed the second, and so on. A kitten usually has eaten enough for one meal after two or three nursing rounds. When a kitten has taken enough formula, it will typically have bubbles around its mouth and an abdomen that is quite rounded, nearly pear-shaped.

Kittens who appear too weak to breastfeed may be hypothermic or have an underlying medical condition.

After each feeding, rub each kitten's whole body with a moist, warm towel. Use short strokes, as its mother would. This exercise cleans the kitten's hair, teaches it how to groom, and provides much-needed socializing. Make sure the kitten is totally dry before returning it to its cage.

Even after feeding, kittens naturally suckle on one another and fingers. Kittens suckling excessively on each other may indicate that the frequency of feedings should be increased. Make sure to separate the littermates if they're suckling on each other close to their genitals. If littermate suckling becomes a problem, separate the kittens, especially in the genital area. Examine each kitten's genitals to check that sucking is not creating any difficulties (redness, irritation, penis hanging out, etc.). Suckling on the genitals can cause the urethra to swell shut and require surgical reopening. If any of these things happen, have a plan for who foster parents should call.

Chapter 3: Kitten Development

Even though they are born with all of their furs, newborn kittens continue to grow and develop after their mother's womb. Kittens go through incredible growth and development in their first week of life. As the litter owner, you should be aware of potential problems and what you can do to help your kittens have a happy and healthy existence.

Physical Development of a Newborn Kitten

A newborn kitten should be around the size of your hand when it is born. It will have the fur, four legs, two ears, and all the other bodily components of an adult cat, but it will not yet be able to perform like an adult cat. Kittens typically weigh roughly 3.5 ounces when they are born, which is the same weight as a deck of cards. Since a kitten's body weight is expected to double within the first week of life, these are handy weights to keep track of a kitten's development. There may be an issue with a kitten's growth if they aren't gaining enough weight. After two days, a kitten's umbilical cord will dry up and fall off, but its eyes and ears will stay shut. There is no other source of warmth, nourishment, or hygiene outside the mother's care for the kitten. As soon as its mother licks it, the baby begins to move about on its belly, cries when hungry, sleep, pees, and poops.

There won't be much difference between a newborn kitten and a one-week-old kitten, but it will get more active as the week progresses. Kittens won't be playing with their littermates just yet, and their primary social engagement will be fighting for a nipple to milk from.

For the first few weeks of your kitten's existence, you'll have to step in and take on the role of mom if it's an orphan or has been neglected by its mother. Nothing can be done about the mother cat caring for her kittens, but there are a few things to look out for anyway. Kittens cannot control their body temperatures until they are a few days old. You may need blankets, an electric heat lamp, a heated pad, and other items to warm your kitten. A kitten's health might suffer if it becomes too chilly. Keep an eye on the kittens for signs of weight increase or loss. These symptoms might signal that the kitten is not eating enough or that something else is amiss. Keep an eye out for bubbles or liquid coming out of the noses. This might result from aspiration or a hole in the roof of the mouth.

Look out for swollen stomachs. This might indicate that a kitten isn't urinating or defecating and need your aid. Ensure the mother cat licks the kittens to encourage them to urinate and defecate regularly. Check the color of the kittens' tongues and gums regularly to ensure they are bright pink. Make certain that each kitten is moving around to sleep and breastfeed. A typical kitten crawls on its tummy in search of a nipple. Examine the mother's nipples to ensure milk is produced for the kittens. A slight pinch of the nipple should cause some milk to ooze out. If the mother cat does not give the kittens enough time to nurse regularly, the kittens will need to be bottle-fed. Some mothers do not breastfeed their kittens.

Newborn kittens have no teeth and rely entirely on cat milk for sustenance. When kittens are young, the mother cat will create colostrum, highly specialized milk. This milk includes unique components known as maternal antibodies, which help protect kittens from infections until their immune systems are fully functional. Kittens must begin feeding soon after birth to ensure that these antibodies are ingested via the colostrum.

A specific cat milk replacement formula should be used to give sufficient nutrition if a kitten is orphaned and has to be bottle-fed.

2 Temporarily, a homemade kitten formula can be utilized. A newborn kitten should ingest around

seven tablespoons per day, eating little quantities every two hours. There is no useful training you can perform with a kitten at this young age. Litter box training will come easily to a kitten, but it should wait until the mother cat is no longer required to motivate the kitten to urinate and defecate.

If the mother cat is there, it is vital to keep her healthy by watching the kittens. Kittens rely on their mothers to feed, clean, stimulate, and keep them warm. Kitten food should be provided to the pregnant mother cat and continued until the kittens are no longer nursing. This will assist offer extra nutrients to the kittens once they are born through the mother's milk. Before getting pregnant, the mother cat should be fully vaccinated so that she may pass on maternal antibodies to her kittens. Make sure the mother cat can relax and breastfeed in a stress-free environment. Nursing and caring for kittens is quite stressful; therefore, unnecessary stress should be avoided.

Mother cats brush their kittens regularly to induce urine and feces. You will be assigned this vital task if you are functioning as their foster parent. This is an essential element of newborn kitten care because tiny orphan kittens cannot pee or defecate without your assistance. Gently massage the kitten's lower belly, genitals, and rectum with a cotton ball/pad bathed in warm water or a fragrance-free baby wipe before and after each meal. Overstimulation will irritate the region, so simply massage enough to induce the kitten to excrete. Keep an eye out for chafing and leftover filth, and keep the kitten warm. During each simulation, kittens should (and nearly usually will) urinate. They must defecate at least once every day. The following are general guidelines:

- ✓ Kittens must be stimulated until they are around three weeks old.
- ✓ Before and after each meal, kittens should be stimulated.

✓ Kittens should urinate and defecate at least once every day.

When kittens reach the age of 3 - 4 weeks, they no longer require assistance in removing bodily waste. Fill a litter box with non-clumping litter or shredded newspaper and place it in the crate or cage. Clumping litter, which can cause litter clumps in their stomachs and respiratory passageways, should not be used on young kittens. You may need to start offering dry kitten food while introducing a litterbox so the kittens may chew on the food rather than the litter. When educating a kitten to use a litterbox, putting its excrement in the box so they can smell it helps a lot. If your kitten defecates on its towel rather than in the box, transfer the excrement to the box rather than entirely wiping it out of the cage.

Kitten Weight Gain and Developmental Milestones

Kittens should acquire around 12 ounces (14 grams) per day or 4 ounces (113 grams) each week. Weigh them using a kitchen or small postal scale simultaneously every day. A lack of weight increase within 24 hours is grounds for worry. Begin syringe feeding the kitten and make a strategy for contacting foster parents. To syringe feed the kitten, prepare the KMR as normal and draw it into a syringe. Place the kitten in the right feeding posture and attach a nipple to the end of the syringe. Try to get the kitten to nurse by gently putting KMR out of the syringe and into its mouth through the nipple. Before inserting an additional formula into its mouth, be sure the baby has swallowed it.

Kitten Developmental Milestones		
Age	Weight	Milestones

Birth	3–3.7 ounces 90–100 grams	The eyes and ears are both closed. 90% of the time, I sleep. Handling is minimal.
2 – 3 days		The umbilical cord falls off.
Four days		It begins to purr.
10 – 14 days	8 ounces 227 grams	Both your eyes and ears should be open. Healthy kittens are round and soft, have pink skin, and rarely cry.
2 – 3 weeks	12 ounces 340 grams	Deciduous incisors emerge and can begin to remove without assistance. Crawling, standing, and playing with littermates will begin. Begin routine handling. Deworming is complete.
Four weeks	1 pound 454 grams	Deciduous canines emerge, begin to walk but lack balance, groom

		themselves, and are thermoregulatory.

Maintain daily care.

They're all set for their first vaccination.

Ready for gruel and maybe dry kitten food introduction. |
| Six weeks | 1.5 pounds

680 grams | Deciduous premolars appear.

Running, playing, using the litterbox, and grooming.

Dry kitten food should be supplemented with canned food.

All set for surgery and adoption (if you can place them at this age). |
| Eight weeks | 2 pounds

907 grams | All are set for surgery and adoption (if you cannot place them at 6 to 7 weeks). |

0 - 1 Week of Age

Feeding: If the kittens have been orphaned, they must be bottle-fed every 2 hours. The kittens should nurse aggressively and compete for nipples if the queen is around. Newborns can breastfeed for up to 46 minutes. If the queen allows it, see kittens nursing at least once a day. Make certain that each kitten is established and fed. A lot of infant crying and activity might suggest an issue with milk flow, quality, or availability. When the queen returns to the box, there should only be a few minutes of fussing before everyone settles down to serious feeding.

Environment: The nest box should be kept at 90 and 85 degrees Celsius. Hypothermia is the greatest danger to newborn kittens.

Development: Kittens should weigh approximately 4 ounces at one week of age and be handled gently. Kittens will properly sleep 90% of the time and eat 10%.

1 - 2 Weeks of Age

Feeding: Continue to bottle feed orphan kittens every 2 to 3 hours until they are full but not bloated.

Environment: Between 80- and 85-degrees Fahrenheit, the nest box's floor temperature should be.

Development: Kittens at two weeks of age weigh about eight ounces. Between 5 and 8 days, the ear canals open. Between 8 and 14 days, the eyes will open. Open slowly, working your way outwards from the nose. There are no distinguishable pupils in the irises of newborn kittens. Thus their eyes seem to be a solid dark blue. The skin of a healthy kitten will be pink, and the cat will be a cuddly size. If you gently pinch them, their skin should bounce back. When you pick up a kitten, it should wriggle vigorously, and when you place it near the mother, it should crawl back to her. Healthy kittens seldom cry. Hold a kitten on its back in your hand to discover its gender. The vulva is a vertical slit above the anus in females; they are quite close together. The penile entrance lies above the anus in men, but they are separated by a high scrotal sac and appear far apart. It is easiest to detect the differences between the sexes if you inspect and compare all kittens.

2 - 3 Weeks of Age

Feeding: Continue to bottle feed orphan kittens every 2 to 3 hours until they are full but not bloated.

Environment: The nest box floor temperature should be between 75- and 80-degrees Fahrenheit.

Development: If there is a queen, she will begin to spend more time away from the nest, though she will not venture far from it. Kittens will weigh between 10 and 12 ounces. Their ears will stand up. Kittens begin crawling about day 18 and can stand by day 21. Even before their teeth come in, kittens will begin to play with each other, chewing ears, tails, and paws. Next, kittens learn to sit and use their paws to contact items. Finally, kittens begin their socializing phase, during which their mother's behavior will heavily impact them for the following six weeks. To socialize kittens further, increase the amount of handling, and get them used to human touch. It is critical not to expose them to anything alarming; youngsters may appear threatening and should be constantly monitored during visits to ensure gentle treatment.

3 - 4 Weeks of Age

Feeding: Continue bottle-feeding orphaned kittens every 3–4 hours and begin weaning. Kittens may begin lapping from a dish at this period.

Environment: From this point on, the floor temperature of the nest box should be 70 – 75oF.

Development: Kittens will weigh between 13 and 16 ounces. Adult eye color will begin to develop, but it may take another 9 to 12 weeks to attain its final hue. Kittens' vision improves, and their eyes begin to resemble and operate like adult cats' eyes.

Kittens will begin to clean themselves, while their mother will continue to handle most heavy cleaning.

4 - 5 Weeks of Age

Feeding: By four weeks, they can normally drink and eat gruel from a shallow dish. While they begin consuming solid meals, weaning should be done gradually, and bottle feeding should be continued every 4 hours. Bring in dry food and drink.

Development: Begin litter training when your puppy is four weeks old. Fill a low box halfway with non-clumping litter or shredded newspaper. Do not introduce the kittens to clumping litter since it is toxic if consumed. Please be patient! The kitten may forget to do this every time or may forget where to find the litter box, but they will rapidly learn. When the kittens first start utilizing their boxes, lavish them with praise. Most will utilize it right away, but they will make mistakes like newborns. To avoid the kittens being disoriented about where the litter box is, put them in an area with a restricted amount of room. Maintain a clean litter box away from their meals.

5 - 6 Weeks of Age

Feeding: Feed gruel four times each day, progressively thickening it. Water and dry food should be provided at all times. Continue weaning if you are fostering a litter with their mother. Some kittens dislike canned food. Mix any meat-flavored human baby food with a little water for picky eaters. Picky eaters often prefer the flavor of the meat. Make sure the brand you choose does not include onion powder, which can be harmful to kittens.

Development: Kittens can begin to explore the room under supervision at around five weeks. They will weigh one pound, and male kittens' testicles will be visible. The most determined and inquisitive kitten will figure out how to escape the nest. The others will soon follow.

Play with your kitties daily! Wear long sleeves and pants since they may play rough and their claws are sharp. They will play "King of the Mountain" from your knees and shoulders if you sit on the floor. This game is both entertaining and beneficial to their health. Some kittens may be scared at first; do not impose on them. You can accustom them to your presence by making phone calls in the center of the room; they hear your voice but do not feel frightened. Make them a part of your domestic activities; familiarize them with the noises of the TV, vacuum cleaner, and other household items.

6 - 7 Weeks of Age

Feeding: Kittens should be able to eat both canned and dry food. Feed the kittens three times every day. If one kitten looks food-obsessed, use a second dish and put plenty of food on the table to ensure everyone is eating. Remember that a kitten at this age has a stomach the size of an acorn, so while they may not eat much in one sitting, they like to feed often throughout the day.

Development: You should have "mini-cats" by now. They will bathe themselves, utilize scratching posts, play games with their toys and you, and many will come when you call. Remember to reintroduce them to their litter box after meals, playtime, and naps. These are the typical times for kittens to use the litter box.

Adoption: It is safe to spay/neuter healthy, vigorous six-week-old kittens and make them available for adoption if you can place them in your community at that age. Check with your state and local animal regulations to see whether this is an option for your facility.

7 - 8 Weeks of Age

Feeding: Provide moist meals 2-3 times per day (each kitten will be eating a little over one can of food per day). Leave a bowl of dry kibble and water out to eat and drink at their leisure. If you have a litter with a mother cat, she should only accept brief nursing sessions, if any at all.

Development: Kittens should weigh 2 pounds by the end of the eighth week and are now small cats.

Adoption: It is time for them to be spayed/neutered and adopted!

Socialization And Bathing

Kittens require exercise at about three weeks to improve muscular and circulatory development and social abilities. If they are not orphaned, they will begin to play with their littermates and learn from their mother. It is best to start touching kittens daily to habituate them to human contact. Play is the best way to help kids develop physically and socially. If kittens are orphaned and do not have a mother to groom them regularly, it is critical to educate them to groom and keep them clean. After each feeding, give kittens a once-over with a barely moist towel. Use short strokes, as a queen would. Kittens frequently become dirty in between cleanings, and it is OK to wash a kitten with warm water under a sink faucet, but just on the regions that require cleaning. A simple "butt bath" would be general enough. Wrap the cat in towels/blankets and a heating pad set on low after bathing. Your body heat is insufficient to keep a chilled kitten warm. Make sure a kitten is totally dry before leaving it.

As challenging as it is, someone has to spend time with kittens to make sure they are well-socialized and friendly with humans before being adopted. Kittens will associate naturally with their mother and littermates if they have them. Another reason to pair solitary, same-age kittens on intake is for socialization. Kittens should be socialized between the ages of 4 and 12 weeks. Kittens begin to play and explore at the age of four weeks. 1 Make sure their cage is filled with toys and entertainment. In addition to classic cat toys, pipe cleaners, toilet paper, and paper towel rolls make excellent play objects. In a foster home, the foster parent should spend some time each day playing with the kittens in the foster room. Ensure kittens in a kitten nursery have some hands-on in-cage socialization time with nursery caretakers. Introducing prospective fosters to the foster parents' resident pets is not suggested during the first two weeks. Allow the kittens to become accustomed to their surroundings before introducing them to other animals. After this time, introducing foster kittens to adult cats and dogs in the home can benefit socialization but should be done with caution and only under supervision.

Prepare a small sink or basin with warm water. If the kitten is unclean, add a little bit of Dawn or baby shampoo to the water. Make the water warm as if you were about to take a bath. To protect the kitten from being chilly, have towels on hand to dry it off quickly. Warm the towels in the dryer ahead of time if feasible. Wear long sleeves and gloves if possible. Kittens may become agitated and scratch. Hold the cat gently by the scruff and support its body with the other hand. This may assist in calming and controlling the kitten. Give the kitten a fast but thorough wash to remove any food or waste. If only its buttocks are unclean, only soak the buttocks, not the entire cat. Rinse the kitten with warm water and cover it with a towel. Rub the kitten dry vigorously. If the first towel gets wet, replace it with a clean, dry towel. Keep the kitten with you, and don't return it until it's entirely dry. While the kitten is drying, put a heating pad around the outside of the towel if necessary.

Whether dry or canned, solid food cannot be consumed by kittens before four weeks. Drinking their mother's milk provides them with the nourishment they need. If its mother is not around, the kitten will rely on you to survive. You may give your newborn kitten a nutritional supplement known as a kitten milk replacer. You mustn't give a kitten the same milk that humans drink. Cow's milk can make cats quite ill. Consult a veterinarian if you are unsure which kitten milk replacer to use. They can assist you in making the appropriate choice.

Refrigeration is not usually necessary for many dry milk substitutes. However, if additional milk is made, it should be refrigerated. Follow these instructions to feed your kitten: Make the formula. Warm the kitten formula until it is slightly warmer than room temperature. Before feeding your cat, check the temperature of the formula. Ensure that the workplace is clean at all times. Hand- and bottle-washing should be done before and after each cat's feeding. In addition, a "kitten gown" is recommended. This might be a robe or a blouse that you wear solely when petting or feeding your cat. Using a kitten robe helps to minimize the transmission of germs.

Feed them slowly. Handle your kitty gently. The kitty should be lying on their stomach close to you. This is the same method they would breastfeed their mother. Try wrapping your cat in a warm towel and placing it on your lap. Find a stance that is agreeable to both of you. Allow them to take the initiative. Place the formula bottle in your kitten's mouth. Allow the kitten to suckle at their speed. If the kitten does not eat immediately away, massage its forehead softly. The rubbing mimics how their mother cleans them and encourages the kitten to feed. Kittens must eat every 3 hours, regardless of the time. Many individuals set the alarm to avoid missing a feeding. This is especially useful at night. You must feed your kitten regularly. Skipping meals or overfeeding might cause diarrhea or serious dehydration in your cat. They should burp them. Burping kittens is the same as burping newborns after eating. Place your kitty on their stomach and gently stroke their back until they burp. If you can't get your kitten to eat for whatever reason, call your veterinarian right away.

What Do Kittens Eat Besides Milk?

You may wean your kitten off the bottle when they are around 3.5 to 4 weeks old. Typically, the procedure begins with delivering your cat formula on a spoon. Later on, begin serving your cat formula on a saucer. Add canned food to the kitten formula in the saucer gradually. Add less and less kitten formula to the canned food on the saucer. If your kitten does not immediately take to the spoon or saucer, you can continue to give the bottle. Monitor your kitten and their feces as you continue through the weaning process to ensure that they digest everything properly. You can gradually introduce more food if your kitten is performing well and isn't having digestive problems (such as loose stool or diarrhea). During this period, it's also crucial to keep your kitten hydrated by providing a dish of fresh water.

Kittens should be housed in a cat carrier that has been covered in many layers of towels. For dogs, a heating pad or heat disc (typically the safer option) combined with a soft fleece blanket can help keep them warm. Make sure your kitten's container is spacious enough to walk away from the heating when they wish to. Maintaining your cat carrier in a secure, warm location away from other pets is critical. If your kitten is chilly, you should warm them up right away. Newborn kittens typically weigh around 3.5 ounces, depending on breed and litter size. Every day, a healthy kitten should gain at least 10 grams. If they aren't growing in size, it's usually a disease symptom. It's critical to keep track of your kitten's weight and how much they consume daily. A gram scale can be used for precision when weighing creatures this tiny. Contact your veterinarian immediately if your kitten isn't eating or growing as planned.

Vets advise not stroking kittens unless necessary while their eyes are still closed. You may check in on them to make sure they're healthy and growing, but try to avoid direct physical contact. The mother kitty will also express how comfortable she is with you touching her offspring. Allow the mother cat and kittens some room if she appears worried or agitated.

Young kittens are unable to go to the restroom on their own. A mother cat would usually clean her kittens to induce urine and bowel movement. To assist your kitten in going to the bathroom, gently touch the belly, genital, and anal areas with a clean, warm, damp cotton ball. Your kitten should be able to use the restroom in less than a minute. After your kitty has finished, gently clean them with a gentle moist towel. You may introduce your kitten to their litter box when they are 3 to 4 weeks old. Add a cotton ball to the procedure like you would when they were younger. This will assist them in determining what to do. Place your cat in their litter box gently and let them get used to it. Continue to practice with them. Assure that their bathroom is in a secure location away from other people and dogs to feel at ease.

While the mother handles most of the job, you should consider yourself her assistant—a co-parent to the infants. Next, keep track of the kittens' weight. It's critical to keep track of their weight so you can ensure they're receiving enough food and staying healthy. If a kitten's weight remains stable or falls, you should be prepared to intervene with extra food. Finally, keep track of the kittens' health. While weight is frequently the best indicator of a kitten's health, you should also watch for any symptoms of sickness or injury. If a kitten looks ill, get immediate medical attention from a veterinarian. Regardless of age or size, newborn kittens may (and should!) get veterinarian treatment. Stop the transmission of illness. When entering their area, wear booties or special socks, especially during their first two weeks with you.

Every day, handle the kittens. It is critical to engage with the kittens for them to develop a passion for humans and solid social skills. Keep up with preventative care. Work with a veterinarian (or your foster coordinator) to ensure that the kittens' deworming, immunization, and other preventative health needs are met. Make sure you've arranged spay/neuter sessions for after the kittens reach the age of 8 weeks. Mama looks after the kittens; you look after Mama! Give Mama plenty of kitten food.

Kitten food has more protein and fat, which the mom will require when feeding her young. Feed your kitten at least three times every day, and provide both wet and dry kitten food. Make a little dish of fresh water available. Please never leave a deep-water dish in a room containing newborn kittens since this can pose a drowning hazard. Fill a low, shallow dish with water.

Mama's teats should be checked every day. Lactating cats can infrequently develop mastitis, a painful breast infection that needs rapid veterinarian attention. Contact a veterinarian right once if you observe any indications of swelling, redness, inflammation, bruising, or pain in the mammary glands. Take care of Mama's medical requirements. If mom becomes unwell, consult with a veterinarian and make sure they know she is nursing kittens before administering any prescription or over-the-counter remedies. Because not all drugs are safe for breastfeeding, please see a veterinarian first. If the mother is friendly, shower her with attention. This phase is simple and enjoyable! Pet her, talk to her lovingly, and encourage her to come out and stretch her legs, sit on your lap, or even play. If mom is wild, only push engagement when essential. Arrange for a spay. Make certain that you sterilize not just the kittens but also the mother cat. It's adorable to see a mom cat care for her kittens, but we don't need more kittens! Spaying mom is best for her physical health, happiness, and the well-being of all kittens.

Typically, the mother cat fulfills all of these responsibilities on her own. You intervene if the mother or kittens appear to be in distress, and you socialize the kittens so they develop used to people. A mother cat's gestation period is normally between 63 and 65 days. You should put up a box for her to become acquainted with during this period. The box's sides should be low enough to allow the mother cat to easily jump in and out, but not so low that the kittens may escape. The mother might give birth in the box, but she could also pick another location.

Examine the kittens soon after delivery. Check to see if the mother cat is stimulating them so they can breathe, urinate, and defecate. She accomplishes this by instantly kissing the infants' faces to get them to breathe. Later, she licks the anal glands to aid excretion. Examine the kittens to see whether they are breastfeeding. Typically, kittens breastfeed every one to two hours. If not, place any non-nursing kittens near the mother cat's breast and brush the kitten's face against it.

Feed a high-quality kitten food to a mother cat when she is pregnant and for a month after she has finished nursing. This provides extra calories and nutrients to the mother cat and her offspring. Food and water should be placed near the mother and kittens. Examine whether the mother and kittens appear to be healthy and prospering. VCA Animal Hospitals suggests taking the mother cat and her kittens to the doctor within 24 hours of birth. The veterinarian can check whether all kittens have been born and whether the mother cat produces adequate milk. You will need to help socialize the kittens to be ready to be petted. When the kittens are two weeks old, begin handling them. Throughout the seventh week, continue to handle and play with the kittens. This is the best time for cats to socialize.

Your cat has given birth to kittens after going through pregnancy. Now is the time for her to care for her kittens, but she cannot nurse them. Mother cats often give birth to kittens and care for them with little or no human interference. However, there may be moments when human assistance is required to help the kittens. What should a worried cat owner do?

Why A Kitten's Mother Can't Nurse

A variety of factors might cause a mother cat's inability to nurse her kittens adequately.

Occasionally, the mother cat may begin feeding and then stop. Alternatively, the mother cat may never begin to nurse. A few of the kittens may be rejected by the mother cat, or all of them may be rejected. She may not only refuse to milk a kitten, but she may also ignore them or act violently when approached by one. Sometimes the issue is not with the mother cat but with a specific kitten or kittens. Smaller kittens or those with serious medical concerns may have more difficulty latching and receiving enough milk from breastfeeding. These issues can be exacerbated in big litters of kittens due to increased competition for time and space to suckle. A mother cat that isn't feeding her kitten has a better chance of doing so if you can figure out why she isn't doing so. The other option is to step in and take care of the kittens yourself. Regardless of the situation, your veterinarian is here to help.

Illness In the Mother Cat

If the mother cat has a health issue, she may be unable to milk her kittens. Mastitis may prevent a woman from breastfeeding. Malnutrition and dehydration affect milk supply. Therefore, it is critical to provide pregnant and lactating cats with constant access to high-quality, nutrient-dense cat chow. Mother cats, especially while nursing newborn kittens, will frequently not even get up, let alone leave the kittens alone; therefore, they must be able to stay hydrated and feed without leaving the nursing area. Any health concerns that make your cat feel ill may prevent her from nursing her babies.

Furthermore, mother cats that are extremely anxious or dangerous may have trouble feeding because they are preoccupied with protecting their babies. It is critical to provide a warm, peaceful, and quiet environment for new moms and litters to connect. A spacious box with nice, clean bedding and easy access to food and water might suffice. The kittens should be touched as little as possible since leaving them alone can be traumatic for the mother. Even though the mother cat looks healthy, it is important to visit your veterinarian if she appears to be having difficulty feeding or if any kittens appear to be very frail, sluggish to gain weight, or have infrequent pee and bowel movements.

Sick Or Deformed Kittens

If a mother cat feels one of her kittens has a health condition, she may refuse to nurse them. Instead, she may remove the ill kitten from the nesting box in an instinctual attempt to safeguard the other kittens. The issue might be a visible congenital deformity, a serious sickness, or something more subtle. Reintroducing a rejected kitten into the nesting box is unlikely to be effective and may further upset the mother. Instead, consult your veterinarian on the best technique to bottle-feed and keep the rejected kitten warm while you arrange for the kitten to be assessed by your veterinarian.

Large Litter of Kittens

Some litters are so enormous that the mother lacks enough teats to feed all of her babies at once. She may also be incapable of producing enough milk to nourish everyone. Larger, stronger kittens may outcompete smaller kittens, and the mother may reject any that become unwell or too weak. In this instance, the best alternative is bottle-feeding any kittens that appear tiny, are nursing less frequently, or are isolated from the rest of the litter. Keep them warm and contact your veterinarian as soon as possible. If they are very underweight and still growing, very young cats may not have adequate energy reserves to make enough milk. Young cats, in most situations, will encounter more hurdles in preserving their health while caring for a litter of kittens. You will need to intervene if you have a young cat with kittens that are not nursing effectively or gaining weight.

Chapter 4: Weaning the Kittens

When a kitten bites its nipple often and hard and can sip formula from fingers, it's ready to wean. Continue bottle feeding kittens throughout the weaning process to provide appropriate nourishment so that they are not excessively stressed. The first stage in weaning is to get the kitten to drink formula from your finger, then a spoon. Put the formula on a flat plate once it has mastered this skill. Mix warm canned kitten food and prepare formula into a thin gruel to introduce the kitten to solid food. Reduce the formula combined with canned food until the kitten eats only the food.

Fill a small dish halfway with food. Some kittens lap straight immediately, while others prefer to suck the gruel off your fingers. Allow them to do so before gradually lowering your finger to the dish.

Kittens may nibble the dish's edge or stroll in the food. It may take two or more meals for them to catch on. If a kitten is not interested in the gruel, gently open its mouth and rub a small amount of the food on its tongue or teeth. Be patient since weaning takes time. Thicken the gruel as the kittens catch on. When kittens consume heavier gruel, fresh water should constantly be accessible in a low spill-resistant bowl. Kittens frequently eat while walking over their food. Before placing the kittens in their cages, make sure they are clean and DRY. Because most weaning kittens are messy eaters, you may not be able to leave gruel or water in their cages for the first several days. Wet kittens lose body warmth quickly.

Signs Of a Cat Rejecting Kittens

A mother cat may reject some or all of her kittens. After helping your cat give birth, observe her behavior to care for any babies she rejects. In some situations, she may care for the rejected kittens. A mother cat may reject some or all of her kittens. After helping your cat give birth, observe her behavior to care for any babies she rejects. In some situations, she may care for the rejected kittens.

Rejection

Depending on the kittens' health, a mother may reject those she believes will not flourish to safeguard the other offspring's survival. Mother cats may reject kittens who have a medical condition or an anatomical impairment. Cats with a big litter of six or more kittens may be unable to nurse all of them, rejecting some to nourish the bulk of the kittens. Furthermore, a mother cat that is unwell or underweight may be unable to care for her kittens, forcing her to reject them.

Behavior

One to two hours after birth, a mother cat should nurse her kittens. After giving birth, a mother produces colostrum, including antibodies that protect and nourish kittens. After that, the mother rejects kittens; she ignores them and won't let them eat. A mother removing one or more kittens from the nest is another rejection sign. She may hiss or bite the kittens.

Kitten Care

A mother may reject a cold-to-the-touch kitten. Massage a chilled kitten's body with a hot water bottle wrapped in a cloth to promote circulation. See whether a chilly kitten's mother will accept it. If a kitten isn't gaining weight or maturing properly, its mother has rejected it. Warm kittens that the mother has separated and refuses to nurse must be bottle-fed; if you return them to the nest, she may reject the entire litter.

Warnings

Kittens are weaned from their mother's milk between four and eight weeks. Because handling kittens under four weeks remove the mother's scent, the mother may reject them. 10 to 15 minutes as mom watches. Examine the rejected kittens and mothers to rule out medical disorders, infections, or after-birth problems. Hand-feed stray kittens.

Transitioning a kitten from mother's milk to solid food is referred to as weaning. The procedure usually begins at four weeks of age and should be completed within eight to 10 weeks. Kittens should be given as much assistance as possible throughout their transition. Place the kittens in a separate place apart from their mother, complete with their food, litter box, and water bowls, for one to two hours each day. The time away encourages them to explore alternatives to their mother's milk and reduces their overall reliance on the mother. Fill the kittens' feeding bowl with a kitten milk substitute. Dip your finger into the milk, then let the kittens suck it off before sliding your finger gently toward the dish. Make sure kitties can reach the bowl. Always give the dish before bottle-feeding bottle-fed kittens.

When kittens lose interest in milk replacement, return them to their mother. Once they are comfortable drinking from a dish, combine wet or dry kitten food with the kitten-milk substitute to make a gruel with the consistency of oatmeal. Gradually reduce the kitten-milk replacement you mix with the kitten food until the kittens can eat solid food. By 5-6 weeks, the milk replacement should be used sparingly to moisten the meal. They should be ready to consume solid kitten food by eight to ten weeks. Be patient while the kittens learn to open and chew their food. Things may become messy when they first stroll into their meal bowls or try to nurse on the food.

Do not start weaning the kittens until they are ready. If you are unsure about a kitten's age, a decent clue is that its eyes are open and capable of focusing, and it can stand on its own. Kittens should have access to their mother during the weaning process if at all feasible. The mother naturally understands what to do when her kittens are weaning, and abrupt separation from the mother might create health and socialization problems. Never offer a kitten cow's milk, which can cause diarrhea and stomach distress in some kittens. Never stick your kitten's snout in a milk dish. This may result in the kitten inhaling the milk and developing pneumonia or other respiratory problems.

How To Bottle Feed Kittens

If the mother cat cannot nurse one or more newborn kittens, it is critical to seek medical attention as quickly as possible. The kittens need to eat every several hours, with the exact frequency depending on age. Bottle-feeding kitten formula helps. Newborn kittens need maternal care. After meals, help them urinate and defecate.

KMR is a popular kitten formula. KMR is sold in cans or cartons in pet shops and online. Other kitten formulas exist. You may give the kitten formula using a tiny kitten feeding bottle. Bottle feeding kittens should be done when lying on their stomachs, not on their backs. Newborn kittens will require bottle feeding every two hours. Gently warm the formula and feed 3-5mL (up to 1 teaspoon) to each kitten every meal. When a kitten unlatches from the bottle, it is most likely full since most kittens stop nursing when they are full.

Furthermore, if you detect formula oozing out of the nose or if the tummy is bloated, you should cease feeding. Since the kittens develop, consult your veterinarian about the appropriate quantities to feed them, as their demands will alter rapidly.

Furthermore, it is critical to keep track of the kittens' weights. Thus they should be weighed regularly with a gram scale. If your cat is expecting babies, keep some kitten formula on hand if the mother has difficulty feeding. If you don't need to bottle-feed, you may always use it to moisten kitten food when they start weaning on solid food. You may also donate the kitten formula to a cat shelter or rescue organization.

After Your Vet Visit, What to Do Next

Kittens should be easily distinguishable from one another so that you can correctly track which kittens have been fed, how much they consume, and monitor their weights and any other symptoms of the disease. The simplest method to tell them distinct is to put collars on them. Use collars that are small enough not to interfere with breastfeeding or movement and fit properly so that little paws don't get trapped. Providing kittens with kitten milk for at least four weeks is a good idea. At three weeks of age, introduce canned kitten food and bottle feeding. Once the kitten is eating on its own, gradually decrease your milk supply. They can tell you what kind of food to provide, how often to feed them, and how to keep them clean and warm.

Cats are mammals. Thus, they nurse their kittens until they are weaned and eating independently. But how long can a cat breastfeed before its milk supply runs out? Cats can become pregnant before a year and remain pregnant for roughly two months. When they are about to give birth, lactation will begin. Cats typically have eight teats, all of which produce milk. Cats who are not pregnant, and occasionally even those spayed, can produce milk, which is false or pseudopregnancy. Hormones in a cat's body regulate this extra milk production. Pregnant cats' teats will swell approximately halfway through pregnancy, but they will not start lactating until a few days before birth. During pregnancy, their hunger will rise to give the extra nourishment that their bodies require to create milk.

When they give birth, the kittens will require the initial milk produced by the mother cat, known as colostrum. After roughly a month of breastfeeding, the kittens will wean themselves from their mother. While the kittens are still nursing from their mother, a liquefied kitten meal should be freely supplied. Over the following six weeks, the kittens will gradually consume more kitten food and nurse less.

During the weaning period, the kitten meal will progress from a liquid to a watered-down canned food, then to standard canned food, moistened kitten kibble, and ultimately hard kibble until it is ready to leave its mother at 3 months of age. If a kitten is eating on its own, you should minimize the amount of time it needs to breastfeed. It is necessary to limit the kitten's access to its mother for a portion of the day if it is eating well on its own but still wants to nurse.

Adequate nutrition is required for a cat to produce adequate milk for all kittens. Cats generally have approximately five kittens in each litter. Still, suppose the litter is unusually large. In that case, the cat may require additional nourishment to assist its body produce enough milk for its young, or the kittens may require supplementation if they aren't receiving enough feeding time with so many litter mates. To meet the increased stress of raising kittens and the energy requirements of breastfeeding, nursing cats should be fed kitten or growth diets high in calories, fat, and calcium. If you are worried about a mother cat's nutritional needs, talk to your veterinarian about what you can do. Weeks three and four of nursing are the most stressful and demanding for the mother cat. The mother cat's body has been consistently producing milk for nearly a month, but it will slow down. Also, less milk will be required because the kittens are weaning off their mother's milk.

As long as kittens are fed, mother cats will continue to nurse. This is useful if you have a litter of orphaned kittens that have been abandoned by their mother and need to be fed, but it is not required if you simply have kittens who are currently eating solid food. When kittens start eating solid food, they normally don't want to nurse. Therefore, the mother cat's milk supply drops substantially. After a few weeks, the milk should be totally dry, but this is a slow process. The teats will remain enlarged and produce milk at first. The milk will cease flowing, the swelling will subside, and the mammary glands should no longer be swollen under the teats after one to two weeks. If your mother cat's teats remain huge, red, and swollen after a week of not nursing, you should consult with your veterinarian. Mastitis is a dangerous and painful illness that may necessitate medicine if left untreated.

Moving a kitten from mother's milk to solid food is known as weaning. It is a vital component of the kitten's growth and must be done correctly and appropriately. The queen, or mother cat, will normally handle kitten weaning independently. But when the queen is having difficulty producing milk or when a litter of kittens is orphaned, we must step in. Here are some pointers for painless and effective kitten weaning.

Before Beginning the Weaning Process

When feasible, kittens should be introduced to mother's milk, especially within the first 12 to 24 hours of life. This is because colostrum, or first milk, contains antibodies that the kitten can only receive at this time. If she cannot provide milk due to mastitis or other problems, another nursing mother may take the kittens if they are near her size.

If you don't have a nursing cat, you can feed a kitten milk replacement formula with a nursing bottle or syringe. In an emergency, Benson suggests blending a cup of whole milk, an egg yolk, a drop of liquid multivitamin, and three Tums in a blender; however, this is just for emergency usage, and you should transition to formula as quickly as possible. Warm the bottle carefully in a cup of hot water before tasting it to ensure that the temperature is correct and has not soured. Keep the unmixed powder in the freezer if you're working with a powder formula. Feed gently but regularly throughout the day, every two to three hours. Don't worry about it at night; they'll wake you up when they're hungry. Allow them to sleep and get some sleep yourself if they're asleep.

Normally, kitten weaning occurs at four weeks of age. "With mom, they'll attempt to take her food, and she'll push them away," Benson explains. You can start a bit early, between three and four weeks, if you're weaning an orphaned kitten. "They're ready when they start biting and chewing on the bottle," adds Benson. You can start introducing kitten food at this stage.

How To Wean Kittens

To begin weaning a kitten, mix kitten food with the formula to familiarize them with the flavor. Next, smear the mixture with your finger about their mouth and let them lick it off. They'll seek it out after they've gotten acclimated to it. Then you may expose them to bowl lapping. Keep an eye on them, so they don't lap too quickly, and never put your face in the bowl, as this might lead you to inhale the mixture and suffer pneumonia. Transition weaned kittens to dry food gradually between the fourth and sixth weeks, supplementing with formula if necessary. Use canned food or dry kitten food mixed with water; start with a lot of water and gradually lessen the quantity as the kitten develops. A general kitten weaning schedule might be:

- **Weeks 4-5:** Mix wet or moistened dry food with a formula to make a slush. If the kitten isn't responding to the new diet, supplement with formula to ensure it receives enough calories.

- **Weeks 5-6:** The weaning kittens should begin nibbling on slightly wet chow.

- **Weeks 6-7:** The kitten weaning process should be finished by now, and they should be consuming all solid food by week seven.

When weaning a kitten onto solid food, it is critical to use kitten-specific food. These diets provide the extra calories, protein, and calcium that growing kittens require. If you have her and her litter under your care, the mother cat can nurse on the same kitten food as the kittens. Warmth must be provided for weaning kittens. Line a high-sided box or pet carrier with towels to make a nest. Benson also suggests layering diapers on top of the towels, clipping the leg openings to help them lie flat. "They're going to become dirty," he predicts, making cleanup much easier. This provides the kittens with lots of heat while also cooling off if they become overheated. Kitten weaning is a natural process; they may just want a little assistance from you. The secret is perseverance and a lot of love.

Why A Mother Cat Rejects Her Kittens

Cats, by nature, make excellent moms. This is proved that even if this is a cat's first litter, she will know exactly what to do with her babies. The feline drive to care for their kittens is so strong that they rarely need humanitarian aid. In reality, our interference can be harmful to the growth of a young cat. However, a mother cat may reject her kittens at times. This might be restricted to just one kitten, but she could reject the entire litter. It might be quite disturbing to observe this happening. This is why, according to AnimalWised, a mother cat rejects her offspring. We explain why they were abandoned and offer advice on what you should do in this scenario.

Is Your Cat a Bad Mother?

Many people assume that if their cat rejects her babies, they are horrible mothers. They may believe the cat opted not to care for her kittens on a whim or due to a lack of love or empathy. However, there is always a rationale for this conduct, even if it is difficult to pinpoint. Although cats may develop intense compassion for other cats, animals, and even humans, we must remember that they are felines. They have cat instincts, habits, and limits that are incomparable to human limitations. Therefore, even though we are tempted to treat our cat as if it were a person, this is both unjust and ineffective for the cat. The circumstances that cause a mother cat to reject her kittens are connected to one of the following:

- ✓ The health of the litter
- ✓ The health of the mother
- ✓ Ability to care for the kittens
- ✓ Stress

These reasons are elaborated on in the following sections. First, however, it is crucial to remember that every mother cat will ultimately appear to reject her kittens. However, this is not rejection; rather, it is an essential aspect of feline growth.

Mother Rejects Kittens to Their Health

The survival instinct is what animals rely on the most. Domestic cats are no different. The cat can sense whether or not the kittens are healthy by using this instinct. This covers whether or whether they were born infected or diseased. They may accomplish this through various means, the most crucial of which is their sense of smell. Remember that a cat's sense of smell is far superior to that of a person. They most likely can detect infections that cause illness.

In rare circumstances, the entire litter may be infected. In these instances, it is pointless for the mother to provide care. More often than not, the sickness or condition will only affect one of the kittens. When difficulties arise during the kitten's gestation, they may develop abnormally. A cat may give birth to a malformed or ill kitten, but how do they separate from the rest of the litter? This might lead to rejection, removal from the nest, or the kitten being eaten. They segregate them because they don't want the sickness to spread to the other kittens. Another reason a mother would eat her kitten is if they have died, and eating them supplies her with extra nutrition.

This may appear cruel to us, yet it is necessary for the animal kingdom. The mother should safeguard the other kittens rather than retain a sick kitten in the nest. Transmission is simple since kittens live in close quarters and share milk from the mother. As human guardians, we may be able to intervene by caring for the kitten. Taking them to a veterinarian implies we might be able to fix the condition, which the mother cannot. After that, we'll have to take care of the kitten's feeding and raising.

Mother Rejects Kittens Due to Her Health

While the vast majority of cat pregnancies are uneventful, issues can occur. Cats can miscarry one or more of their litters for various reasons. Some cats may acquire an illness during pregnancy or have an underlying medical condition aggravated by the procedure. Some will be healthy, but difficulties in delivery might cause serious injury.

For example, suppose one of the kittens twists while being born. Even if the kitten is born successfully, the mother might be damaged in certain situations. When this occurs, the mother would probably abandon the kittens because she is too frail to care for them. If the problem is an infectious illness, she may reject them to keep them from being contaminated.

If you see that the mother has rejected the kittens, yet she is weak or showing disease symptoms, you should take them to a veterinarian. You will also be responsible for the care and feeding of the kittens unless the mother cat is rapidly returned to health so that she may resume parenting. Even in the latter instance, she might not.

Kittens Abandoned Due to Carelessness

Even though most cats prefer to take care of their kittens, there are a few exceptions. They may not know how to feed or care for them, and they may choose to leave them because of their lack of concern. The reasons behind this may be difficult to determine, particularly if we do not know the past. If the mother cat was abandoned as a kitten, she might be at a loss about what to do. Trauma or prior negative experiences may also indicate a lack of capacity to care for their babies adequately. If this happens, you can try to teach them by bringing the kittens closer to her teats to feed. Mother cats will transfer their newborn kittens for various reasons, which keep them safe from imagined danger. These can be tough for the mother cat to learn, but you may be able to 'jump start' her instinct, and she will take control. It will almost certainly need some patience.

There are various cases where a mother will have a big litter. The size of the litter is determined by the cat's size, although anything larger than 5 or 6 is considered huge. Even though some cats can care for all of them, others may not have enough milk to do so or may not be able to do so. In such instances, the mother may reject one or more weak kittens. We must give the mother a secure environment that includes all she requires for these and other reasons.

Mother Cat Rejects Kittens Due to Stress

The cat will be aware that she is ready to give birth near the conclusion of her pregnancy. They will instinctively choose a secure and comfortable location to give birth to her litter. This location is remote and distant from potential risks. The mother cat, like humans, may get apprehensive or agitated due to the upcoming delivery. This is a delicate moment, and our actions can impact their well-being. We can worsen their tension by trying to overwhelm them with attention or physical manipulation. If we try to modify their preferred birthing location, make unnecessary noise, or otherwise disrupt their sense of security, we may unintentionally contribute to the cat leaving her babies.

You can aid by giving blankets, limiting noise, and maintaining a comfortable temperature. Aside from that, and a safe distance, you should leave the mother cat alone. You should only shift the nesting site if you are aware of a threat, but the cat is not. We must also give the mother room and time after the litter is born. Then, her instincts will control her, and she should have no trouble caring for the kittens. Although the kittens are adorable, the mother will become stressed if we come in and take them up too often. Cats who exhibit indications of stress before delivery are more likely to be agitated when parenting their kittens. We should only intervene if one or more kittens have been rejected or if there is a clear issue.

What Should You Do If a Mother Refuses Her Kittens?

As we've already said, there are several reasons why a mother cat could reject her kittens. If there is a problem with the mother or kittens, you must take them to the veterinarian. It's their job to know what to do if the problem can be fixed. We may have to feed the kittens if the mother refuses to return them.

To properly feed a newborn kitten, you will need this book. The kitten will eventually need to be weaned onto solid food, and our kitten weaning guide can assist you with this.

There is nothing more wonderful than a mother cat looking after her kittens. This is nature's way, yet occasionally something goes awry. A mother cat may appear to lose interest in her kittens and reject one or more of them or even abandon them when they most need her. This is tough to grasp. Why would a mother cat abandon her kittens? To find answers to this topic, we visited credible sources and feline behavior specialists to learn about the probable reasons why some female cats refuse to accept their kittens. Cat Time specialists give some light on this terrible event.

Some female cats reach physical maturity before developing parental instincts. Cats age at varying speeds, just as some people do, assuming they ever exhibit these innate tendencies. Because they are still kittens, some mom cats have no idea what they are doing. Although it is uncommon, it does occur, so don't blame her. Instead, provide her emotional support while attempting to care for the kittens on your own or seek the guidance of an animal health specialist to learn how to care for the kittens.

If a cat has a big litter, she might not have enough milk to nourish all kittens. In addition, it might be taxing on her body. As a result, she may reject a couple of the kittens to feed the rest of them. If this is likely to happen, it generally shows up within the first 24 hours of delivery. Observing new mothers with large litters is a good idea so that you may intervene if required.

Mother cats will occasionally reject a physically deformed kitten. Although these kittens are healthy except for visual flaws, the mother will refuse to care for them. It is advisable to remove the kitten rather than attempt to persuade the mother to adopt him. She may reject and abandon all of the kittens.

Cats are odd animals, and you can only push them so far before they walk away and do their own thing, even if it doesn't make sense. Don't assume she has abandoned them if you find kittens born outside and the mother is not around. She may be hunting. If she doesn't, she may have been hurt or killed and may be unable to return to the nest to care for her kids.

Mastitis, an infection of the mammary glands, can occur in nursing mother cats. This is a painful condition characterized by nipple hardness and swelling. The region may become inflamed and uncomfortable to the point that she can't bear it anymore. She might not even be rejecting her kittens. It is important to visit a veterinarian for assistance in alleviating her illness. If the mother cat is ill, she may be unable to care for the kittens. If she appears tired or has had a rough labor, it is important to seek expert medical help. She needs an evaluation to determine the nature of the issue and, if required, treatment.

Mother cats that are malnourished both before and after giving birth to a litter of kittens may be unable to provide milk. This may force her to reject the entire litter of kittens. If she cannot feed them, she may grow frustrated and leave. Allowing them to suckle when there is no milk coming out is painful. According to The Nest, there are four symptoms that a mother cat is rejecting her kittens. The first is annoyance or tension. It's not a good sign if she's upset with the kittens instead of loving and washing them. The second sign is if the kittens are always crying. The crying will persist until she pays to heed. If it doesn't stop, she'll ignore them. The third indicator that the mother rejects her kittens is if she kicks one or more of them out of the nest and refuses to care for them. If your cat does this, any attempts to coerce her into accepting the kitten may result in her rejecting all of them. The fourth indicator is a mother cat who is aggressive toward her kittens.

Cats are complex creatures, and it may be difficult to comprehend why they do what they do. If your mom's cat shows indications of rejecting her baby, there is nothing you can do to change her mind. The best course of action is to take the kitten or kittens she has denied and keep them warm while feeding them the kitten milk substitute. It is feasible to raise them to the point where they can consume solid food independently, but it is a labor of love. Raising young kittens takes a lot of time and work, but it will be worth it when they start wandering about and eating kitten food on their own.

What Are Maternal Behavior Problems?

Nature usually takes its course when a mother cat produces kittens, and the mother will automatically and naturally care for her offspring. Maternal behavior difficulties are a broad set of concerns of some deviation from the regular course of events. The most prevalent maternal behavior issues in cats are the mother cat's lack of maternal conduct for her babies and excessive maternal behavior when the mother cat does not have kittens.

There are several causes of maternal behavior issues in cats. Researchers have discovered that specific genes influence different forms of mothering behavior in cats. Mother cats may lack the natural impulse to mother their litter in the absence or presence of a faulty mothering-related gene. Hormonal changes also cause maternal behavioral disorders. A hormonal imbalance can lead a cat to have a fake pregnancy, in which she exhibits symptoms of having kittens, including birthing symptoms such as contractions, yet she is not pregnant. Stress can also be a source of problems. If a mother cat feels threatened by other cats, humans, loud noises, or other stressful conditions, she may abandon her kittens or develop hostile tendencies against them. First-time mothers may be more prone to behavioral issues.

It would be a simple observational exercise to detect the presence of material behavior issues in your cat. The veterinarian's major emphasis on diagnosis will be establishing the underlying reason for the abnormal behavior. As with most ailments, a complete physical exam at your veterinarian's clinic will precede the diagnosis. You should bring the mother cat and any kittens for this appointment. It is critical to provide a detailed history of your cat's behavior, including any escalation or changes. You should also offer as much information as possible about any outside stressors or other important data about your cat's living environment.

Your veterinarian will evaluate your cat for any evident physical problems. Your veterinarian will order a full blood panel to rule out any infection or hormonal disorders causing the symptoms. Your veterinarian may also prescribe a urinalysis to screen for the presence of post-pregnancy hormones.

Treatment Of Maternal Behavior Problems in Cats

Treatment of maternal behavior issues in cats can range from management to pharmaceutical, depending on the severity of your cat's behavior and the prevalence of underlying diseases. The most prevalent type of therapy is management. This can entail extracting aggressive mother cats from their babies, hand-feeding them, or locating a surrogate mother for the kittens. The signs of excessive maternal behavior usually go away after a few days. Your veterinarian may recommend hormone therapy to reduce or eliminate signs like breastfeeding or uterine contractions in extreme situations. Spaying may be advised for cats exhibiting excessive maternal behavior since it has been demonstrated to reduce this condition in most animals.

Effective management of your cat's maternal behavior issues is critical to your cat's overall recovery and the healthy development of any kittens. Owner monitoring can help you manage your cat's hostility or inattentiveness toward her kittens. You may need to restrain your cat until the kittens are old enough to be weaned from their mother. In the event of inattentive moms who are not aggressive, monitoring and being there with the mother cat and her kittens may be sufficient to enable feedings and cleanings.

Your mother cat should also have a peaceful, quiet place to lay her eggs. This will soothe the mother and may lessen or eliminate any nervous behavior like abandonment or excessive movement of the kittens. Other cats or animals should be kept apart from the mother cat. Cats with maternal behavior disorders recover quite well with proper care. After the kittens have grown, the symptoms usually go away. Spaying cats with maternal behavior disorders is a good idea since the concerns are likely to reoccur during subsequent pregnancies.

If Kitty is pregnant, you may be considering a pleasant setting for her to give birth, but she may have other plans. Cats frequently have their views about safety and choose their birthing locations, which are often out of sight and difficult to access. After all, they're adorable, lively, and quite cuddly. They're virtually impossible to resist. This is why many mommy cats will make every effort to keep them away from humans. It's not personal, but Kitty's primary responsibility as a mother is to keep her children safe. If you set aside a space for her to have her kittens, don't get insulted if she declines; she's doing what she feels is best for her kids.

Don't take it personally if Kitty moves her kittens. If she suspects they'll be in danger, she'll relocate them to a safer location. If the location where she gave birth is too crowded — too bright, noisy, or crowded — she is more likely to shift the kittens. Cats enjoy a peaceful, safe environment, especially in the first several weeks. Remember that kittens can't see, hear, or move around very well during the first week or two of their lives. Kitty spends the first three weeks of their life caring for their needs, feeding and grooming them, and keeping an eye on them as they understand their environment. At this point, it's better to accept her maternal instincts.

If you wish to assist, make sure she has easy access to fresh food and water and is in a warm location. Check-in daily to ensure that everyone is in good health. Keep other people (particularly other animals, youngsters, and strangers) away from her refuge so she doesn't have to change her thoughts again. Otherwise, let her mothering instincts take over. Experts appear to agree that waiting three weeks before handling kittens is preferable. It is critical to socialize the kittens to be at ease among people. If you do this too quickly, Kitty could think you've interfered and relocated them again. If you have little children, keep them away from Kitty and her babies unless you are there. Kittens aren't able to stand on their own until they're around six weeks old.

Prepare the materials you'll need for bottle feeding before bringing the kitten home. Wrap the carrier with an old small/baby blanket to keep the kittens warm, but leave some room or holes to allow air in and prevent suffocating. Kittens do not like being chilly. So, ensure that they are warm and, if not, gently warm them up before feeding. Touch the pad of a kitten's foot, ears, or lips to see whether it is chilly. If any of these feel chilly, it's probably because the kitten's temperature is lower than normal.

Extremely low temperatures can be fatal to kittens and should be treated quickly. Warm-up a kitten by enveloping it in a thick little blanket or towel, hugging it close, or gently stroking it with your warmed palms. Powdered kitten milk replacement formulations are preferable to canned ones when feeding newborn kittens. Several powdered formulations are available in pet stores, both online and offline. High-quality powdered formulas help reduce diarrhea, are nutrient-dense, and adore kittens. Unless you are certain of the kitten's age, you should read the blog entry on identifying the ages of kittens before feeding. This would allow you to care for and provide for it properly.

In addition to being unable to ingest and digest solid food, newborn kittens cannot evacuate waste (urination and feces) without assistance. As a result, after each 24-hour feeding, you should stimulate them to assist them in passing waste. It is preferable to do this every three hours (feeding and elimination). Kittens should also not be overfed or have their meals skipped since this has been linked to issues such as diarrhea and dehydration. While dealing with the cleanliness and other care requirements of a kitten with diarrhea might be difficult for you, it can be harmful to the young cat. Therefore, it would be great if you had a veterinarian examine the kitten as soon as the diarrhea began and avoided any probable triggers as much as possible.

It is possible even while feline moms are unlikely to leave their kittens. However, desertion should not be confused with other causes that may lead a cat to abandon her litter for an extended time. I reviewed some of the various reasons a cat may be "abandoned" and what you may do if you are certain that the mother cat did abandon the kitten. Finally, I must emphasize the need to exercise caution while dealing with an abandoned kitten. Even though extended absence from the litter may indicate desertion, you still want to ensure the cat's mother is not around to avoid attacks. Another reason to be cautious is to avoid illness transmission to other pets or humans in the home. Before bringing the cat home, do your homework and check all the boxes. We should also highlight that kitten moms may cease to nurse their kittens after four weeks. This is normal because they are typically transitioned from milk to solid food between the fourth and eighth weeks of life. If you are unclear about the age of the abandoned kitten, go to the page on determining a kitten's age so that you can appropriately feed and care for it.

Chapter 5: Litter Training

Kittens like to urinate themselves in soil or sand. If you expose them to one, they'll gladly use a litter box instead of your carpet. It's critical to find the right box for your kitten and encourage her to use it, but unlike a dog, you won't need to "litter train" a cat. You should not have to educate your cat on using a litter box; instinct will usually take over. You must supply a suitable, easily accessible litter box.

Purchasing Supplies

Choose a big litter box. Small boxes are available for little kittens, but because kittens grow so quickly, you'll need to replace the litter box shortly after introducing it. When you replace a litter box, you must retrain the kitten, so start with a box you want to use for a long time. Kittens may easily enter huge litter boxes if one side is low enough for them to step inside. If you discover a nice box but aren't sure if the kitten will be able to climb inside, construct a tiny ramp out of plywood or similar flat material with a strong grip. Attach it to the edge of the litter box with duct tape and take it off when the kitten is large enough to get inside without it.

Consider a litter box that is enclosed. Some litter boxes are surrounded by an enclosure (or top). The covered litter box can contain the litter for an energetic kicker/digger and may reduce odors if the box is in a compact living area. The cage also provides some cats with a sense of security. Ensure the enclosed litter box is spacious enough to allow cats to turn around comfortably. Most cats have a behavioral urge to sniff their excrement and subsequently bury them, so the box should accommodate this. When first introduced to enclosed boxes, some cats do not enjoy them. You may make the transition easier by removing the swinging door until your cat is comfortable with the box.

Purchase kitten litter. There are wide varieties of litter to choose from, and most of them are suitable for most juvenile or adult cats. Because dust can irritate cats' lungs, choose a litter that is as dust-free as possible. You should consider the following criteria: do not use clumping cat litter for kittens. If they ingest it, it clumps together in their stomach and can cause a catastrophic impact. If possible, use the unscented litter. Kittens and cats may dislike scented litter; if the aroma is too strong, they may use the toilet elsewhere.

Furthermore, some fragrances may irritate a cat's nose and eyes and create respiratory difficulties in cats. Think of scoopable trash. Scoopable litter has grown in popularity since it makes eliminating the kitten's waste so simple. There is some risk that a cat may become ill from eating scoopable litter. However, there has been little or no proof of this happening. Next, choose a commonly accessible litter. Some cats develop a preference for a certain litter and may not perceive the tray as a toilet unless it includes their preferred litter. Finally, a scooper and a drop cloth are required.

Introducing The Kitten to The Litter Box

Place the box somewhere quiet. Place it in a low-traffic section of your home, such as the kitchen or entry hall. The best litter box placement is easily accessible, provides many seclusions, and is devoid of loud noises that might startle a kitten. Though a laundry room is a common site since it receives less activity than other parts of most homes, the unexpected noises that a washer or dryer might produce while switching cycles may shock a kitty and cause her to be afraid of using the box. The litter box should be placed where the kitten spends a significant amount of time. The litter box should be visible to the kitten most of the time so that she may use it if necessary. Kittens and cats want to be alone. They may begin discharging themselves under the sofa or in another inconvenient location if they don't have it. Daily movement of the box from one room to another may confuse the kitten and result in disasters. It may also be advantageous to position the kitten's food dish near the litter box, as most cats are afraid to use the potty where they eat. Finally, place the kitten in the litter box that has been emptied. Place the kitten in the box as soon as you get her home so she may become acclimated to the smell and feel of the kitty litter. Allow her a few minutes there, even if she doesn't use the restroom the first time. Continue to put the kitten in the box after she feeds, wakes up, or at any other moment you anticipate she may need to discharge herself.

Furthermore, if she squats anyplace other than the litter box, immediately place her in it. Some kittens grasp the purpose of the litter box right away and don't need any more litter training. You should avoid attempting to "teach" the kitten the digging action that cats use to bury their waste since it may startle her, so resist the urge to grasp her paws and assist her in digging into the litter until she gets the hang of it.

Use praise rather than punishment. As the kitten becomes accustomed to the litter box and begins to use it as her potty, reward her by caressing her and making soothing sounds. Do not chastise her while in the box, or she may begin to associate it with punishment. Kittens dislike having their noses touched in a mess they've produced outside the litter box. To discipline a kitten, never slap or shout at her. It will just make her fearful of you. Make enough litter boxes. If feasible, have one litter box for each cat in your home and an extra litter box. One kitten, for example, should ideally have two litter box alternatives. You should supply four litter boxes if you have three cats.

Consider a term of imprisonment. You may wish to restrict her to limited space for the first few weeks after bringing a kitten into your house. This can help her gradually adjust to her new surroundings, easily access her litter box, and limit or contain accident locations. You may wish to restrict the kitten to an area without carpet to make cleaning up accidents easier if they occur. Keep the kitten's litter box, food, and bedding at separate ends of the confinement space.

Keeping Your Kitten Comfortable

Every day, clean the litter. Kittens dislike going to the bathroom in filthy places. If you don't replace the litter, the cat may find a cleaner spot to do her business, such as the carpet. First, scoop the trash out of the litter box, place it in a tiny baggie, seal the bag, and toss it away. During the first several weeks, you can leave a tiny amount of excrement in the litter box (changing it periodically). This teaches the kitten what the box is for. Next, clean the whole litter box regularly. You will need to empty the litter pan and thoroughly clean it once a week. After emptying the pan, wash it with a non-hazardous cleaning solution (or warm soapy water), rinse it, dry it, and replace it with new litter. Due to the simplicity of eliminating the cat's waste might be tempting to leave scoopable litter for longer than one week. Even scoopable litter, however, must be thoroughly emptied and replenished regularly. Finally, thoroughly clean the accident scene. If your kitten or cat goes to the toilet outside of the litter box, thoroughly clean the area to remove all evidence of urine or feces. This should assist in minimizing the number of accidents in the same region.

Consider getting rid of any huge potted plants in your home. If your cat begins to use the dirt in your potted plants as a toilet, you may need to remove them or cover the dirt with foil while litter training. Kittens bury their excrement naturally. Therefore, they may be drawn to dirt or sandy places. Ensure the litter box is the only location cats want to relieve themselves in the house. Feed the kitten regularly. This will assist you in predicting when she will need to use the litter box. Kittens often have a bowel movement around 20 minutes after feeding. When you suspect she needs to go, take her to the box and let her climb inside.

Chapter-6: Get Ready for Adoption

First Vet Visit for Your Kitten

It's always wonderful to welcome a new kitten into the household. It might be a planned and much-anticipated occasion, or it can be a sudden adoption or rescue. In addition to purchasing all new essentials such as food, plates, and litter boxes, plan time for the initial veterinarian appointment and regular checks. The initial visit to the veterinarian may identify underlying disorders that affect you, your family, and other pets. Some ailments might quickly worsen, so it's essential to determine whether your cat needs special care straight early. You mustn't put this off for everyone's health in your family, including the new kitten.

Before You Go

A veterinarian should examine your new kitten as soon as possible to determine its overall health. There is no specific age for the initial vet appointment. However, it is advised that the kitten be examined within 24 to 72 hours of adoption. If you already have cats, you should take the new kitten to the vet before bringing it home. Your new kitten may be suffering from a disease that you are unaware of. A pre-adoption vet visit may be impossible due to circumstances such as a rescued kitten or other urgent adoption. In this case, confine the new newcomer in a bathroom or similar location away from your other pets. The litter box, food dish, and water bowl should all be provided for the kitten. This reduces the possibility of illness or parasite transmission to any resident cats.

What You Need

You'll need to have certain items ready before the initial exam, whether you go immediately to the doctor after picking up your new kitten or at home after a day or two.

- ✓ Any information or documentation supplied by the shelter or breeder
- ✓ Make a list of any worries you have concerning the kitten.
- ✓ Cat carrier
- ✓ Stool sample
- ✓ Cat Treats

Your veterinarian must know whether and what sorts of treatments and immunizations have already been administered to the kitten. Bring adoption documentation to your kitten's first vet visit. If it is not possible, write down what you were taught so you don't forget. Next, call the person from whom you adopted the kitten and ask any questions you may have. The staff and veterinarian will ask you about your kitten's background and do a physical checkup. Your kitten will be weighed and may require a blood test to screen for illnesses. They will also search for other parasites like fleas and mites.

The veterinarian will examine your kitten's eyes, ears, lips, skin, coat, and entire body. This includes feeling the organs in the abdomen and listening to the heart and lungs with a stethoscope. For intestinal parasites, a stool sample may be collected. In addition, it is frequently advised to carry a fecal sample with you if feasible. For maximum health, weaning time, and socialization, kittens should be adopted at 8 to 10 weeks (or even longer). If your kitten is young, especially six weeks or under, the vet will need to examine the kitten's nutrition and hydration condition and offer any necessary supplements.

Vaccinations And Treatments

The first vaccine for a kitten is usually administered between 6 and 9 weeks. If your kitten is sneezing or has other health issues, the vet will not vaccinate it until it is well. Kitten immunization boosters will be required every three weeks until your kitten reaches the age of 16 to 20 weeks. The rabies vaccination is usually administered at the final kitten checkup. At each appointment, your kitten will be given a dewormer to treat common kitten intestinal parasites such as roundworms. Make an effort to plan these sessions so that your kitten does not miss any necessary immunizations or treatments. Your veterinarian will go through your kitten's health and preventative care requirements, such as heartworm prevention and flea and tick control. Vaccine and preventative measures recommendations will be given based on your kitten's surroundings. Your veterinarian may also help you with litter box training, diet, spay/neuter, and behavioral issues.

Your veterinarian should be informed if you have any queries or concerns about your cat's medical condition. If your kitten becomes ill at any moment, you must immediately call your veterinarian. Catastrophic illnesses may develop swiftly in kittens. In a non-emergency circumstance, establishing a bond with your vet and a new pet is always easier. Knowing the clinic hours and who to contact in an emergency will put you ahead of the game.

What to Expect at the First Vet Visit for Your Kitten

When you bring a freshly acquired kitten home, you must have it examined by a veterinarian as soon as possible. This is important for your kitten's health and guarantees that it does not share any major infectious diseases. Ideally, your kitten should be evaluated before bringing it home, but if it looks healthy, you should aim to get it seen by a vet within 48 hours. If the kitten exhibits any signs of sickness, such as wet eyes, sneezing, trouble breathing, or inability to eat, it should be examined as soon as possible. Your kitten should not be allowed to interact with other cats until a veterinarian has given the all-clear.

What Does a Physical Exam Consist Of?

Your veterinarian will do a thorough hands-on physical examination of your kitten to detect physical problems, just like an adult cat would. This examination will include- Examining the interior of your kitten's mouth—baby teeth, the tongue, and the roof of the mouth will be particularly scrutinized. Taking your kitten's temperature- A cat's normal rectal temperature ranges from 99 to 102 degrees Fahrenheit. If your kitten's temperature is either high or low, this might indicate a problem. Palpating your kitten's abdomen- Your veterinarian will gently feel your kitten's abdomen for any abnormalities. Listening to your kitten's heart and lungs- A cat's heartbeat should have a regular rhythm with no murmurs. The lungs should be clean, and only air should pass through them. Testing your kitten's muscles and joints for mobility- Your veterinarian will feel your kitten's legs, particularly their knees, to ensure that everything is in order. They may observe your kitten walking about to ensure that it has a normal stride. Examining your kitten's eyes- An ophthalmoscope may be used to inspect your kitten's eyes. Your veterinarian will also search for indications of sickness, such as wet or crusty eyes. Checking your cat's ears for mites- A kitten with ear mites will have heavy, black debris in its ears. Because ear mites are prevalent in kittens, your veterinarian may swab a sample from within the ear to look for minute mites. Combing your kitten's fur for fleas- Fleas prey on cats of all ages. Fleas can be found with a flea comb.

What Lab Tests Will Your Kitten Need?

1. **Fecal analysis:** You will almost certainly be requested to bring a fecal sample from your kitten to your veterinarian. The veterinary team will test the fecal sample to look for parasites such as intestinal worms, giardia, and other possible problems. Because not all

intestinal parasites show up on fecal tests, and many kittens have them, your doctor may give your kitten a de-worming medicine at each appointment. In addition, many parasites may be transmitted to humans. Thus, it is essential to remove them from your cat.

2. **Blood tests:** Every new cat should be tested for FeLV and FIV regardless of its age or whether it lives with other cats, according to the American Association of Feline Practitioners (AAFP). Testing for FeLV and FIV in kittens under nine weeks is less reliable; therefore, your veterinarian may suggest you wait until they are nine weeks old before getting the test done. If your new kitten is infected with FeLV or FIV, you should keep your existing cats at a distance until they have been vaccinated.

Most jurisdictions require cats to have at least one rabies vaccine, which is not given to your kitten until older. Other vaccinations, such as rhinotracheitis, calicivirus, and panleukopenia, should also be discussed with your veterinarian. Vaccines must be administered at specified ages and intervals to be effective.

How To Separate Kittens Properly from A Mother Cat for Adoption

As a cat owner, you should check that all parties involved—the kitten, mother, and new owner—are happy before relocating your cat or adopting a kitten. The most crucial thing is to wait until the kittens mature — ideally 12-13 weeks. The mother cat will normally adjust to the separation swiftly if you do. Kittens, on the other hand, will take a little longer. To make each kitten's transition as simple as possible, prepare the kitten ahead of time, ensure she is weaned, gently introduce her to her new home, and use extreme caution if introducing her into a home with an existing cat.

Preparing A Kitten for Separation

When the kittens are around 12 weeks old, they will be separated from their mother. To help kittens interact correctly, most experts recommend delaying weaning until 12-13 weeks after birth. Socialization is how kittens investigate their environment and accept what they discover normally. A well-socialized kitten is confident, brave, and friendly. Separating a kitten too soon from its mother, on the other hand, may result in poor learning capabilities and an aggressive temperament. A kitten begins to learn about three weeks and continues to sponge until 12-14 weeks of age, when her ability to adjust to the unknown begins to wane. A kitten will benefit immensely from learning from its mother until 12 weeks old. If re-homing is delayed for an extended time, the kitten is far more likely to be afraid and hide from the new owner. Before separating the kitten from her mother, make sure she has learned to use the litter pan. By the time they're 12 weeks old, most kittens will have mastered the art of using the litter pan. Before adopting a kitten, be sure she has learned this critical skill from her mother.

Introduce the aroma of the new owner to the cat. Scent teaches kittens a lot about their surroundings. They can smell their mother, littermates, and nest. This understanding can help a kitten adjust to life apart from her mother. This may be accomplished by having the new owner bring an old T-shirt that smells like the individual. When the cat moves in, she will be familiar with one of the odors, making her feel safer. Introduce the kitten's scent to an existing cat in the new household.

Similarly, if the house already has a cat, offer him some bedding with the kitten's scent. This will offer the existing cat a smell 'handshake' before meeting the new kitten. Again, this will alleviate any possible tension between the two animals.

Around four weeks of age, begin weaning the kitten off her mother's milk. Kittens must be weaned off of their mothers' milk and onto solid meals before adoption, both for their health and to avoid harmful behaviors like "wool sucking," cats chew and suck on objects like cloth. The mother cat will wean her kittens independently, generally between 8 and 10 weeks. Next, take the kitten away from its mother. At four weeks, you can start leaving the kitten alone for a few hours at a time. Provide her with her litter box, food, and water bowl.

Teach the kitten to lap milk using a shallow dish and kitten milk replacer. Place your finger just beneath the surface of a glass of milk. The kitten will try to suckle your finger but eventually decide that it is simpler to lap at your finger rather than suck it. Giving the kitten cow's milk may disturb their digestive system.

Solid food should be introduced. When the kitten can drink milk on its own, it is appropriate to introduce wet solid meals. Begin with a gruel-like consistency and gradually reduce moisture until the kitten eats dry food by 8-10 weeks. To prepare the gruel, combine dry or canned cat food with a milk replacer until it resembles oatmeal. Reduce the amount of milk substitute slightly each day until the meal is very faintly moistened by week 6. The kitten should start eating dry food between weeks 8 and 10.

Introducing The Kitten to Its New Home

Take some bedding from your kitten's previous residence. Make plans to bring a towel or blanket from your new kitten's previous home. A familiar aroma will make the transition much simpler. Put this blanket or towel in your cat's carrier on the way home and keep it there for him to nap on. Bring home your new kitten in a carrier. The carrier will protect your cat and make them feel more comfortable. Use a different pet's carrier since the smell of another animal might be unpleasant for the kitten. Make a haven for the kitten. Make sure your kitty has her modest area or space. It should be discreet and out of the way. Kittens need a bed, water, kitten food, a litter box, a scratching post, and safe toys. Consider lining the cat's bed with an old hoodie to help the cat get acclimated to your scent. The space or surroundings should provide places to hide. Allow your kitty to explore her den at her own pace. Put her carrier in the room, open the door and let her out when she's ready. Leave the carrier in the room as an additional hiding spot.

For the first week, limit your engagement with the cat. You will most likely want to hold and pet your kitten all the time. Don't. Your kitten will need time to acclimate to her surroundings, including their people. Then, slowly introduce each member of your family one at a time, enabling your kitten to get used to your presence. Nobody should handle a cat under five years old. Cats should avoid this area because of the threat it poses to them.

Bringing your kitten home after settling into her den is the next step. Cats are more comfortable in their rooms when they eat, drink, and use their litter boxes frequently, so you may gradually introduce them to the rest of the house. Next, allow her to roam freely in a room with her carrier open. For at least a few hours after exploring, bring your kitty back to her den and then continue your journey. It's best to gently pick up and put your cat back down on the floor if she attempts to climb on something you don't want to. You'll have an easier time establishing no-go zones for your cat if you do this right away.

To prevent giving her health problems during the separation, continue to feed the kitten the food she was weaned on. Giving the cat its favorite meal will give comfort and prevent an upset stomach caused by the bacteria in her intestines adjusting to a new food. Plan ahead of time and ask the person selling you the kitten what sort of food they've been giving it so you can have that food available when the kitten comes.

To alleviate the kitten's anxiousness, consider utilizing a plug-in pheromone diffuser. Cats emit facial pheromones (chemical messages) that they rub on safe surfaces, such as their bed, a chair, or leg. Plug-in diffusers spray a synthetic version of these pheromones, alerting cats that they are in a safe environment. They last around 30 days, giving you plenty of time to console your cat as she adjusts to her new surroundings. Feliway is the most prevalent type of pheromone diffuser. It might be in the form of a spray or a plug-in device that emits pheromones automatically.

Gradually introduce the new kitten to an existing cat in the house. If the kitten has been well socialized and placed in the new household between 12 and 13 weeks, she should adjust smoothly. However, if there is already another cat in the house, you should introduce the two felines gradually. For example, place the kitten's den in an area your current cat does not visit. This allows the elder cat to become aware of the presence of another feline in his area in a nonthreatening manner since she is not vying for his food or good resting locations.

Begin with a perfume introduction. Under the new kitten's room door, your cats will sniff at each other. You may even switch bedding between the two animals to get them acquainted with one other's smell. It's also a good idea to brush one cat and then the other to mix their odors. To alleviate your resident cat's uneasiness, pay additional attention to him. Ignoring him and focusing all of your attention on the cat will lead to difficulties. Feed the cats on each side of the entryway to the new kitten. This will cause each cat to identify the other cat's scent with something positive: food. Have the cats switch places once the kitten has become accustomed to his new lair. Put your existing cat in the kitten's room while the new kitten is introduced to the rest of the home. This will allow the cats to investigate each other's odors in new environments.

Helping The Mother Cat Manage Separation

Separate the kittens from the mother gradually. It's better if the queen cat's milk supply runs down gradually. Her mammary glands may become uncomfortably engorged if you remove all of her kittens. Next, remove everything that has been sprayed with the kittens' fragrance. The mother cat may appear to prowl about the home hunting for her kittens due to the remaining fragrance of her kittens. Providing the mother with clean bedding and eradicating any traces of the kittens' scent is crucial once they've been adopted. Her impulse to hunt will decrease as their scent disappears from the environment, and she will return to her usual routine.

Know that the queen cat will rapidly recover from her separation. Nature has programmed the mother to make her kittens self-sufficient for them to live, and as part of this process, she begins to separate herself from the kittens to stand on their own feet.

Rehoming the kittens just speeds up the process. The queen cat will normally only exhibit indications of worry for a day or two before reverting to her normal patterns if her kittens are mature enough when they go (ideally 12-13 weeks) and their odors are eliminated.

How To Adopt a Kitten

The sight of a kitten is intoxicating. They are also naturally clean, will grow up to be independent, and do not require housebreaking. They are popular as adopted pets for this and other reasons. However, you can't just walk down to the shelter and adopt on the spur of the moment. Becoming a kitten parent entails analyzing your preparation and preparing your house before the adoption procedure. When you meet and bond with your new little pet, you'll realize the effort was worthwhile. Check to see whether you can accept a cat into your household. This should go without saying, yet far too many individuals leave their pets because they were unaware that their living circumstances were unsuitable for pets. If you are a tenant, go over the provisions of your lease that pertain to companion animals. Whether they are permitted, check with your landlord to see if your rent will be raised. Check that no one in your family is allergic to cats. Before bringing a furry buddy into the house, be sure they can control their allergies. You might also think about adopting an allergy-friendly breed. These cats produce less dander than other breeds and are less prone to cause allergies. However, an entirely hypoallergenic cat does not exist.

Consider the obligations. While adult cats are self-sufficient, kittens do not like to be left alone for lengthy periods. If you live alone, consider who will feed your cat if you have to work late or travel for work. Consider whether you're prepared to clean the litter box at least once a day and groom the cat regularly. Even with frequent brushing, cats shed regularly. This implies you should vacuum once or twice a week. If you don't live alone, ask your housemates (significant other, children, flatmates, etc.) if they're prepared to share the tasks. Feedings and brushings might be added to your children's tasks.

Make certain that you have enough money. Many shelters provide the first check-up, microchipping, and spaying/neutering. You will, however, need to budget for regular tests and vaccines. If you intend to allow your cat outside, you must spend on heartworm protection. Buying cat food, treats and litter are all expenses that must be considered. If you must be away from home frequently, you should also consider the expense of a reputable cat sitter. Finally, consider insuring your pet against unexpected medical costs.

Conclusion

When you anticipated your bundle of joy, you could have read a stack of books. But are you aware of what occurs when your cat becomes pregnant? Don't stuff pickles and ice cream into Fluffy's dish. Simply treat them like the queens that they are. "Queening" refers to how a mother cat prepares to give birth to kittens. Cats who have not been sterilized can get pregnant as early as four months if they have not been spayed. During the spring and early fall, queens may be in heat every two to three weeks, making them eager to mate. Pregnancy in a cat typically lasts 63-65 days. So a six-month-old cat can mate and give birth to kittens. In cats, pregnancy "morning sickness" is extremely rare; however, they can lose interest in food or vomit. If this persists, get them seen by a veterinarian. Hormone surges and changes in the uterus can cause tiredness. It will take a few weeks for this phase to pass completely. Cats aren't the only ones that may need more calories and food during pregnancy. They'll eat an additional 1.5 times their normal calorie intake throughout their pregnancy. Pregnant cats should be fed special food designed for them, which your veterinarian can prescribe, during pregnancy and when nursing their kittens. Your cat's vaccination schedule should be followed since viruses can affect kittens before birth. Before delivering a vaccine, deworming/flea treatment, or medicine to a pregnant cat, you should consult with your veterinarian. Pregnant women should not receive most vaccines. As a result, it is best to vaccinate your dog before you want to breed it. Make your house a comfortable place for the new baby to stay when they arrive. Avoid having your cat go into labor by not allowing them to go outside as much.

Two weeks before the due date, your cat may begin acting abnormally as they enter nesting mode. You may help them by looking about your house for a good place to give birth. The mother and her kittens will be happy in a medium-sized box with a low opening filled with newspapers, old towels, and soft blankets. A private part of your house is the best location for the nesting box. Let your pregnant cat visit it regularly before the delivery to make her feel more at peace. Cats are creatures of habit, and even if you do all you can to aid them, they'll still do what they want. If that's what they want, they'll give birth in a laundry basket, behind a garbage can, or at the back of your closet. If you see your cat nesting, take her to the doctor for one last pregnancy visit. The vet will explain what to do if there's an emergency during the birth. The cat's body temperature drops below 100 degrees Fahrenheit, warning that the delivery is imminent. These kittens won't be long for you to get to know!

Your kitty is aware that you are the Food Person. She also understands that you are the Potty Person, Laundry Person, and Spa Attendant. You may easily forget about the other responsibilities as a replacement mother when caring for a bottle baby.

You're also the headmaster; get out your mortarboard, teaching the life lessons that Mom can't anymore.

Baby kittens, like children, rely on their surroundings to create their personalities, influence their conduct, and give boundaries. Because kitten brains are built to absorb these things before they're fully weaned, Mom and her siblings are usually in charge of educating her. While it may appear to be a good idea from a health aspect, isolating a kitten is the worst thing you can properly do to a cat's mental health. A kitten's growth is vital between two and seven weeks when she learns important socializing behaviors from her mother. During this critical period, she learns what to be afraid of and what is safe. If she is not exposed to a wide range of people, animals, and events, she will likely develop a life-long dread of that missing ingredient.

Without her mother or classmates, a kitten reared on her own only learns the lessons taught to her by her foster mother. That individual is transformed into the center of their universe. The kitten loses all independence and has the potential to become an overbearing and controlling cat. Over-attachment is a common issue among such kittens. Kittens mimic their siblings' social and predatory characteristics. "If I bite too hard, he squeals," I quickly discover. Without sufficient socialization alone, orphans develop into violent cats; some become chronic adult biters. (Not the tiny love bites, but the hard, almost-draw-blood chomps downs.) In the absence of other kittens, the orphan engages in regular hunting activities. She learns that biting the fingers that feed her is appropriate behavior if she is permitted. Nipping is cute when she's four weeks old, but it's not so cute when she's four years old and 14 pounds. It's a difficult habit to overcome later in life, and the kitten's behavior may persist when she moves to her new home. These poor felines frequently wind themselves at animal shelters. You must inform her that her fingers and toes are always off-limits. Any biting results in a stern "No!" and the game is over. You get to your feet and walk away. Maintain consistency. Get everyone on board for the sake of the cat.

Never strike or physically punish your kitty. She won't see the link between her actions and the slap on the nose. She will simply learn that you are a wild person who goes mad abruptly and should not be trusted. Another technique to halt improper conduct is distracting her with a toy or item. Allow your nice, tolerant cat (healthy and up to date on immunizations) to teach the kitten proper behaviors. They do, after all, communicate in the same language. Your orphan will learn catness if she is exposed to other cats. And, unlike you, your grown cat will punish her for being too rough.

You widen her universe by introducing her to a range of compassionate individuals with goodies and engaging toys. Kittens that have grown up with gentle dogs should have little trouble adjusting to a new home with friendly dogs. If other animals cannot be included in the curriculum, give her plenty of engaging toys, exercise, sociability, and a plush animal to wrestle with. Two or three energetic play sessions each day, chasing prey objects on a string, let her kitten energy drain and fulfill her predatory aggressiveness. (Always keep string toys out of reach of her, as eating string can result in life-threatening injuries.) The most important thing you can give her is good to play. Constructively harnessing that seemingly limitless energy source contributes to her and her family's ability to live a joyful and busy life together.

<-END->

Printed in Great Britain
by Amazon